By Ernest Havemann

«————————————————————»

THEY WENT TO COLLEGE
(*with Patricia Salter West*)
I NEVER THOUGHT WE'D MAKE IT
(*with George Love*)

THE AGE
OF
PSYCHOLOGY

by

Ernest Havemann

SIMON AND SCHUSTER
NEW YORK, 1957

The psychology quiz in Chapter I is reprinted by permission from *Introduction to Psychology* by Clifford T. Morgan. Copyright, 1956, McGraw-Hill Book Company, Inc.

FIRST PRINTING

« CONTENTS »

« FOREWORD »

PSYCHOLOGY *was already an established part of the curriculum when I entered college in 1928. It was not, however, by any means so respectable as it is today. The chemistry and physics professors looked down their noses at it as a johnny-come-lately science which was probably not a real science at all. The English and philosophy professors snubbed it as a lowbrow substitute for the nobler truths of Shakespeare and Socrates.*

I took a course in psychology anyway, partly by accident and partly from stubbornness, and was entranced by what I found. Every young person is full of all sorts of deep wonderment about his senses, his mind and his emotions—and for the first time I began to get an inkling of how these things work. I was fascinated to discover how light waves hit the retina of the eye and cause us to see; how little invisible electrical patterns get traced into our nervous systems and enable us to learn; how some people get into trouble and become case histories in a textbook of abnormal psychology or psychiatry. Before long I was working on a Ph.D., determined to study and teach psychology the rest of my life.

At that point my interest collided with an earlier ambition, to become a journalist, and came off second best. I *held a $1,000-a-year fellowship in the graduate school of Washington University and gave it up to earn $750 my first year as a depression-time reporter for the St. Louis* Star-Times. *This has enabled me to claim—with what my friends probably consider boring frequency—that I am the only man alive who lost money going to work. It has also led to a career with which I have always been perfectly happy— except insofar as it has deprived me of my other love.*

By a rare good stroke of fortune, I had the opportunity some months ago to combine my two interests. Henry R. Luce, the editor-in-chief of Life Magazine, *had the idea for a series on the general subject of psychology, psychiatry and psychoanalysis, explained in terms which the reader could understand without necessarily having any prior background. I was called in to tackle this rather formidable assignment, not as an expert, for nobody at the magazine knew that I had ever studied psychology, but simply as a writer known for a certain foolhardy optimism and a willingness to do a little homework.*

I did the homework and now I have my Ph.D. in psychology, not as a formal title, of course, but to my own satisfaction. I had my own private tutors. One was Dr. Clifford T. Morgan of The Johns Hopkins University, former chairman there of the Department of Psychology, consulting editor of psychological publications for the McGraw-Hill Book Company, and author of the standard textbook Introduction to Psychology. *The other was Dr. Fredrick C. Redlich, a distinguished psychiatrist who studied with the Freudian group in his native Vienna and is now chairman of the Department of Psychiatry in the Yale University School of Medicine.*

Dr. Morgan was consultant to Life *on the articles dealing with psychology, Dr. Redlich for those dealing with psychiatry and analysis. I need hardly say that without them it would have been impossible for a layman like me to write the* Life *series, which appeared in the issues of January 7 through February 4, 1957, or this book, which is based on the magazine articles.*

Besides Dr. Redlich and Dr. Morgan, my thanks go to the many other psychologists, psychiatrists and psychoanalysts who gave generously of their time and counsel. I am also indebted to the editors of Life *for their helpful journalistic advice and the privilege of reprinting material from their pages, and to the researchers for the magazine, notably Maya Pines and Kimball Frease.*

ERNEST HAVEMANN

Glen Rock, New Jersey, 1957

CHAPTER ONE

The Psychology-Psychiatry Boom

AFTER getting up the other day, John Jones, American, shaved with a razor he had bought on the strength of a magazine ad approved by the head psychologist of an advertising agency. At his breakfast table, in his morning newspaper, he read two columns of psychological fact and advice. One told him that women were absolutely not more intuitive than men, all popular opinion to the contrary notwithstanding. The other invited him to find his "happiness quotient" by answering a series of ten questions. He then drove to work, guided by road signs painted yellow and black because a psychologist once discovered that these colors make for easier reading. At the plant he walked past the office of the company psychiatrist, where he would have been free to go in and seek counsel had he felt especially disturbed about anything that morning, and got right to work at his job, to which he had been promoted after taking a series of psychological tests.

Among his other duties this particular morning was a conference with an industrial psychologist who had been retained to advise on the company's pending contract negotiations with the union. At noon, over his lunch, he read two more psychological columns in his afternoon paper, one telling him how to improve his relations with his mother-in-law, the other advising a letter writer that her errant husband probably had a mother fixation. He also read in his favorite gossip column that one of his pet movie actresses, about to go on location in Africa, was taking along her personal psychoanalyst lest she lapse into another of her spells of melancholy. In the afternoon he faced an office crisis because a psychological research firm, hired to poll the public's opinion of his company, had found a marked loss of goodwill in the preceding six months. When he went home at night he found his family in something of a dither because his youngest son had been called in for a conference with the school psychologist: subject matter, repeated impudence to the second-grade teacher. To relax he took his wife to a movie, where the first half of the double feature took place in a mental institution and the second half contained a sort of farcical psychoanalyst strictly for the laughs. They arrived home just in time for the late TV newscast, which informed them that government officials were in a hassle over how much money to spend on psychological warfare.

2

All these things might have happened to any American this week. They could not have happened in any previous generation and they could not have happened even this week in any other country, for widespread use of psychology as an applied science of everyday living is brand-new and strictly American. The birth of modern psychology took place less than 100 years ago, of psychoanalysis scarcely more than 50. In many parts of the world all knowledge of them is still restricted to the college classroom or the doctor's office. But in the United States, for better or worse, this is the age of psychology and psychoanalysis as much as it is the age of chemistry or the atom bomb.

In many ways the practitioners of psychology are too intriguing for their own good. Every scrap of information about them is eagerly gobbled up, whether authentic or not, so that a good deal of what the public has come to believe is utterly wrong. Psychiatrists often find that new patients have misconceptions which hamper their treatment for months. Psychology professors starting a freshman class usually find that they must sweep their students' minds free of a great deal of misinformation before they can begin any constructive teaching. Dr. Clifford T. Morgan, consultant on psychology for the *Life* Magazine series on which this book is based, once drew up a little true-false quiz for his beginning students—and found that most of them got the answers completely wrong. The quiz, taken from Dr. Morgan's fine textbook *Introduction to Psychology*, is reprinted here so that readers may try it for themselves:

	True	False
1. Only human beings, not animals, have the capacity to think.	☐	☐
2. Much of human behavior is instinctive.	☐	☐
3. Slow learners remember better than fast learners.	☐	☐
4. Intelligent people form most opinions by logical reasoning.	☐	☐
5. You can size up a person very well in an interview.	☐	☐
6. When one is working for several hours, it is better to take a few long rests than several short ones.	☐	☐
7. The study of mathematics exercises the mind so that a person can think more logically in other subjects.	☐	☐
8. There is a clear distinction between the normal person and one who is mentally ill.	☐	☐
9. Prejudices are mainly due to lack of information.	☐	☐
10. The feature of a job that is most important to employees is the pay they get for their work.	☐	☐
11. It is possible to classify people fairly well into introverts and extroverts.	☐	☐
12. Punishment is an effective way of eliminating undesirable behavior in children.	☐	☐
13. By watching closely a person's expression, you can tell quite well the emotion he is experiencing.	☐	☐
14. The higher one sets his goals in life, the more he is likely to accomplish and the happier he will be.	☐	☐
15. If a person is honest with you, he can usually tell you what his motives are.	☐	☐

4

Every one of these statements, the psychologists say, is false. Yet most of Dr. Morgan's freshman students believed the statements were true—and the reader can certainly be forgiven if he thought so too.

Psychology is probably misunderstood for the same reason it is so popular: it deals with a subject on which people have always considered themselves to be authorities. The layman has never boggled at expressing and swallowing the most sweeping judgments on human nature and its aberrations. One indication is the widespread popularity of such age-old saws as "Early to bed," "All work and no play," "Still water runs deep" and the like, many of which, by the way, are mutually contradictory. The psychologist, the psychiatrist and the psychoanalyst all operate within the general area delineated by the old saws about the nature of man, with these differences:

The *psychologist* searches for a scientific understanding of how people see and hear, his interests thereby overlapping those of the physiologist. He also tries to find out how they learn, how they feel and express their emotions and how they get along (or do not) with their fellow men, at which point he and the sociologist are on somewhat similar ground. The psychologist once was chiefly a research specialist and teacher; he began by applying scientific methods of observation and measurement to human behavior, and instructing others in what he found. Many psychologists are still interested only in "pure science"—that is, in fact and theory. A majority of them, however, have branched out into applied psychology, attempting to use their knowledge to help people live happier and more efficient lives. Some of them, for example, counsel young people on what

5

vocations to choose or advise businessmen on how to provide better working conditions for their employees. Quite a number of them work at what is called clinical psychology, which is an attempt to help individuals who have emotional problems and personality maladjustments.

The *psychiatrist* is also interested in human psychology, but as a physician attempting to understand and treat the people in whom something has gone wrong. He specializes in the care of what used to be called insanity (but what he now calls psychosis, the victims being known as psychotics) and less severe mental disorders (which he calls neuroses, the victims being called neurotics). Most psychiatrists work in public and private hospitals. About two thirds of them also have private practices, in which they treat patients whose difficulties are not severe enough to require hospitalization.

The *psychoanalyst* is a special kind of psychiatrist. He too is a physician who treats the mentally ill. (At least he usually is a physician, though there are some excellent "lay analysts" who have never taken an M.D.) But he uses a special type of treatment originally developed by Dr. Sigmund Freud: the analyst spends hundreds of hours listening to the patient discuss his past and present life, his dreams and his daydreams—until finally the patient's pattern of hidden or "unconscious" problems emerges to the point where it can be straightened out.

We all have friends nowadays who can tell us, using such psychological or psychiatric terms as extrovert, introvert, frustration, tension, sublimation and psychosomatic, exactly what is wrong with the way we get along with our wives, rear our children, deal with our bosses and approach our hobbies. A great many people embrace and spout this kind of psychological lingo without really knowing the first thing about it. And for this reason a lot of other people have come to hate the very mention of psychology without understanding it either.

Another cause of confusion is the fact that a lot of people have jumped on the psychology bandwagon without the proper qualifications or caution. Most of the popular books, magazine articles and newspaper columns containing psychological "fact" and advice absolutely appall most professional psychologists and psychiatrists. A good case in point is the column called "Know Thyself," which appears in the New York *Post* and the Philadelphia *Daily News*. Readers of "Know Thyself" are invited to score themselves every day on questionnaires purporting to determine such questions as these: "Do you have social poise?" "Are your emotions under control?" and "How happy are you?" It would be perfectly possible, in the opinion of most psychologists, to score 100 per cent on such a test on Monday—and on Tuesday have a complete nervous collapse. As for the numerous columns which supposedly clear up any human problem in a hundred well-chosen words, one psychoanalyst has said: "This is the most amazing thing in the world. The columnist reads a letter from a perfect stranger and that very day states the exact nature of his problem and recommends a cure. Most of us would be happy if we could analyze the problem in years of intensive work—and we'd have to leave any 'cure' up to the patient himself."

Yet, right or wrong, serious or frivolous, practically

anything relating to psychology and psychiatry finds a big audience. Nine out of ten of the major U. S. daily newspapers carry at least one column of psychological lore. If the syndicate figures are to be believed, a column called "Child Behavior" has a circulation of 9.5 million; "The Worry Clinic," 19 million; "Mirror of Your Mind," 20 million. "Let's Explore Your Mind," a question and answer column illustrated with cartoons, is said to have a circulation of 21 million and to draw nearly a million requests a year for the 10¢ and 15¢ pamphlets offered by the column under such titles as *How to Find Your Happiness Cycle, Facing the Facts of Married Life* and *How to Manage Your Feelings and Emotions.* Psychiatry has even invaded the newspaper comic strips. In *Rex Morgan, M.D.,* there have been episodes concerning an old man with senile dementia and a young husband who became a victim of paranoia and had to be hustled off to a mental hospital after nearly killing his wife. (*Rex Morgan, M.D.,* it so happens, is written for his own amusement and profit by a practicing psychiatrist in Toledo, Ohio.)

Books of psychology or psychiatry for the layman often become best-sellers. A writer named Lucy Freeman told the story of her own psychoanalysis in *Fight Against Fears,* which sold 35,000 hard-cover copies and 330,000 in a paperback edition. She followed this with *Hope for the Troubled,* a discussion of the various types of psychological assistance, which has sold 140,000 copies. (There is an even greater sale of those perennial best-sellers, the self-help books—like Dr. Norman Vincent Peale's *The Power of Positive Thinking* or Harry Overstreet's *The Mature*

Mind—but strictly speaking these books have to be classed as inspirational rather than psychological, though many of them also expound psychology in keeping with the trend of the times.) Even books designed for professional psychologists and psychiatrists—and consequently full of the most complex and esoteric kind of language—are having a big sale among laymen. *The Basic Writings of Sigmund Freud*, published as a 1,000-page Modern Library Giant at $2.45, has sold over a quarter of a million copies.

So familiar is the psychiatrist that in the entertainment world he has become a stock character. Of the plays running on Broadway during one recent season, no fewer than five had psychiatrists in their cast of characters—more than had warmhearted Irish cops, charming drunks or comic housemaids. In the movies the heroes of even light comedies like *The Seven Year Itch* and *That Certain Feeling* have received advice from psychoanalysts, and a psychoanalyst was actually the hero of *Oh Men, Oh Women*. A study made a year ago by a psychiatrist showed that about one movie out of every ten contained either a psychiatrist or a psychiatric problem. Nobody would venture even to try to count the psychiatric references in humorous cartoons and the jokes of nightclub comedians.

The center of psychology used to be Germany, where much of the original work was done, in close collaboration with the physiologists, on the question of how human beings receive their sensory impressions of the outside world. The capital of psychoanalysis used to be Freud's native Vienna. But now the United States has more psychologists and psychiatrists, engaged in more types of inquiry and activity, than all the rest of the world put together. It certainly provides the biggest and most eager audience for psychology.

Why should this be? Nobody really knows, but those who are interested in the field have speculated as follows: In the first place, psychology is an irreverent science, ready to question man's fondest beliefs about himself and his society; it cannot flourish in a totalitarian state or in a nation which has grown too stuffy and self-important. It assumes—especially in its practical applications such as aptitude testing and human engineering—that all men are more than mere cogs, and worthy of study and consideration. It is of course a luxury, and needs a high standard of living to support it. In its therapeutic aspects, which are based on the premise that something can be done about mental illness and human unhappiness in general, it fits in with the general optimism of the United States. It also takes a kindly and permissive attitude toward children, who are the special pets of American culture.

Psychiatrists have sometimes speculated that another reason for the great demand for their services in America may be the revolution in sexual morals which has taken place here in the last forty years. The revolution is often attributed to psychoanalysis, but this is just another of the erroneous notions which are so rife in this field. Psychoanalysts do not advocate sexual promiscuity and usually take a dim view of divorce. Freud himself was a solid, middle-class monogamist, who considered the eighteenth-century novel *Tom Jones* too shocking for his bride-to-be to read, and his successors have also tended to be as circumspect in their moral standards as they are lurid in their theoretical concepts. They had nothing to do with the American sexual revolution, which, as is proved by the Kinsey studies, took place before they had much influence—and they often feel that perhaps fewer people would turn to them were it not for the confusion and conflicts that the revolution has created.

Certainly the services of the psychologist and the psychiatrist are badly needed by humanity, and the vogue of psychology in America cannot be considered a mere fad. Mental disease is, and has probably always been, one of mankind's greatest problems. Almost everybody has seen examples of it—a relative, friend, business associate or girl down the block who has to be put into a mental institution, sometimes never to emerge again. On any given day in the United States there are a little more than 1.4 million people in hospitals, and of this number more than half, or around 750,000, are mental patients. High as it is, this figure only begins to tell the story. We do not have nearly enough hospitals and hospital beds to take care of our mental patients, and it has been estimated that around 300,000 more patients urgently require hospitalization but do not get it.

In addition mental illness and personality disturbance play a large role in causing suicides, crime, juvenile delinquency, narcotics addiction and problem drinking, the last of which, say the authorities, affects some 3.8 million Americans at the present time. Trying to tackle this vast problem, psychiatrists cannot help viewing with amazement and mild envy the amount of effort and public concern that goes into raising money for research in such diseases as muscular dystrophy (100,000 victims in the U. S.) and polio (38,000 cases a year).

As for the neuroses, the minor forms of mental disturbance which make so many people jittery and miserable without necessarily disqualifying them from the daily business of living, the total defies any real estimate. The more conservative psychoanalysts maintain as a rule of thumb that about a third of all adults are neurotic. A substantial number, however, believe that practically everybody is neurotic except people who have been successfully analyzed. A good deal depends upon the definition, which is not easy to make. No two experts are likely to agree on what constitutes neuroticism, or how seriously neurotic any given person is.

In general, a neurotic person may be defined as one who suffers unreasonable fears or anxieties. The symptoms may take such varied forms as tension, depression, insomnia, lethargy, or fear of elevators or crowds. In the days before laymen began talking with such self-assurance about "introversion" and "inferiority complexes," the neurotic person used to be considered "nervous" or "high-strung" and if he finally collapsed under the weight of his burdens he was said to suffer a "nervous breakdown." But this sort of person constitutes only part of the problem. Some of the most neurotic people are never recognized as such except by the experts, even in this psychologically sophisticated day. The hail-fellow-well-met, the chronic joiner, the life of the party, though he seems perfectly happy to the layman, may to the psychologist be gregarious only because his own unbearable tensions force him to act so. The successful businessman, climbing to the top over every obstacle in the most admirable old Horatio Alger tradition, may be driven to success by his own inward lack of confidence in himself. Perhaps the best measure of the amount of neuroticism in our society is this: every expert knows that there are even fewer completely happy people than there seem to be.

Some of the experts think that civilization itself is the villain—that the human brain is simply unable to cope with the noise, speed and complexity of modern life, particularly in a freewheeling democratic country like the United States where the individual is confronted day after day with all the bewildering advantages of freedom and is under strong competitive pressure to make the most of them.

Certainly the average person has to make a tremendous number of adjustments in his lifetime. In his youth he may be a high school football hero, widely admired in his home town. He then goes on to a college where he is not good enough to make the team, gets no adulation whatever and finds himself thrown part of the time among professors who seem to admire only the mind and part of the time among young ladies who most admire the social graces such as dancing. He takes a job where he must show a modest eagerness and deference to the boss, then is made foreman of a bunch of workmen who will respect him only if he acts tough, then moves along to a higher executive position where the slightest raising of the voice may be considered gauche. In addition he is closely involved emotionally with a wife who knows nothing of his business world and children whom he can never decide whether to indulge or to discipline. He also has to get along in such varied roles as a member of the board of governors at his country club (where he is not too well thought of because he can't break a hundred), a Boy Scout leader (where his stamina on a weekend camping trip is suspect) and a deacon of the church (where piety is the most admired trait). If he sometimes feels as if he is flying into small pieces—not an uncommon neurotic complaint—who can blame him?

While civilization certainly has its pressures, some of the experts think it may not so much create aberrations as merely expose them. A recent incident in Canada may be in point. A psychotic who had escaped from a mental hospital was captured after 18 months of freedom, which he had spent living alone in a forest at the edge of some farming country. Out of metal foraged from junk heaps he had managed to fashion himself a lathe, and with this lathe he had made a rifle and a pistol for hunting game. He had also built a mill for grinding grain that he stole at night from the nearby fields. During most of mankind's history, certainly all through the long era when communication was mostly by grunts, a man of such ingenuity and resourcefulness would have been considered a great leader, if not a genius, no matter how peculiarly he behaved in other respects. Even within recorded history there are numerous examples of famous men who were in all likelihood completely off their rockers by today's standards. A good many successful empire builders were probably (like their unsuccessful modern counterpart, Hitler) the victims of paranoia (delusions of persecution and grandeur). A good many prophets were doubtless plagued by hallucinations.

The modern psychiatrist, treating mental problems as a disease rather than an invasion of demons or willful misbehavior, first appeared on the medical scene around 1800. Early treatment of psychotics was not very successful, however; the work was generally unpleasant and the number of doctors willing to devote themselves to such an unorthodox specialty grew very slowly. Certainly the psychiatrist had very little fame or influence among the general public until Freud came along with the concept of psychoanalysis, which he developed around 1900 after profound study of his own neurotic problems as well as those of his patients. Freud's theories, shunned at first by his own fellow doctors, gradually began to attract attention among medical scholars, became a topic of discussion among intellectuals all over the world and suddenly appeared before the U. S. public eye about a quarter century ago.

Eugene O'Neill's *Strange Interlude* and *Mourning Becomes Electra,* two of the best-known plays around 1930, brought some of the basic Freudian theories to the stage and gave psychoanalysis a great burst of notoriety. Ever since then, psychoanalysis has had an especially great influence on the "communicators" of our society: the writers, playwrights, artists, actors and cartoonists. Partly this is a matter of geography. Psychoanalysis, like the lively arts, has centered in New York and to a lesser extent in Hollywood. Partly it is a matter of economics. The successful novelist, playwright or actor, much more than the average man, has the money and time to try analysis when his problems get out of hand. Also, Freud's writings offer a dramatic and challenging new interpretation of mankind, which is something the artist is always seeking. Many authors have been analyzed; some have read Freud and understood him; some have read Freud and hardly understood a word—but all in all there is hardly an author practicing today whose work has not been influenced by psychoanalysis. Thus Freud has had hundreds of the most effective possible press agents working for him free.

As for the psychologist, he got his first great boost toward public acceptance in World War I, when it was discovered that he could perform what were then considered wonders in measuring the intelligence of draftees and predicting how much if anything they would be capable of learning. Even in 1920, however, only about 400 men and women were enrolled in the American Psychological Association, and practically all of these were teaching in colleges. By 1940 there were 3,000 members and quite a few were leaving the campus to practice applied psychology elsewhere. During World War II psychology enjoyed its greatest upsurge as the government demanded the answers to a lot of research problems in testing, training and propaganda. Since the government was willing to pay for the experiments and for the training of new psychologists to work on them, the new science underwent a tremendous expansion. Today A.P.A. has 16,000 members. Half of them teach and the other half have moved into all sorts of other activities. They work as personnel men and efficiency experts for industry; as vocational counselors in colleges, the Veterans Administration and the U. S. Employment Service; as designers of tests for the Army; as counselors on children's problems in public and private schools; as pollsters of public opinion; and as specialists in the treatment of the mentally disturbed in clinics and hospitals.

From time to time there have been rather bitter disputes among the psychologists, the psychoanalysts and the non-analytical psychiatrists. College students of a generation or two ago may recall that practically every freshman psychology textbook used to contain a disparaging reference to psychoanalysis, which was regarded as unprovable in the laboratory and therefore rank nonsense. The psychoanalysts, for their part, considered the psychologists to be the drab experts of the obvious, picking at the superficial aspects of the human personality. If anything drew the psychologists and psychoanalysts together in those quarrelsome days, it was their mutual distaste for most nonanalytical psychiatrists.

Both the psychologists and psychoanalysts believed and still believe in treating mental illnesses as primarily functional, that is, as a matter of mixed-up mental processes and pressures susceptible of being unraveled by the right kind of talk between the patient and the expert. Many nonanalytic psychiatrists, on the other hand, have tended to believe that mental aberrations would someday be traced to physical causes and cured by doses of the proper medicine, just as pneumonia and syphilis can be cured with penicillin. It was the nonanalytic psychiatrists who were mostly responsible in the past for the widespread use of such techniques as frontal lobotomy and electric-shock treatment, and who today have the most faith in the widely publicized tranquilizing drugs.

These intramural frictions still send up an occasional spark, but not nearly so often as formerly. Except among a few diehards in each camp, there is very little talk these days about "schools" of psychology and psychiatry, and most people working in these fields are moving in more or less the same direction. It is becoming quite common in many hospitals and clinics for a psychiatrist or a psychoanalyst to work with a psychologist as a therapeutic team, often with a social worker as a third member.

At the same time the whole general field of psychology and psychiatry, which grievously shocked a good many of our grandparents and aroused the antagonism of many philosophers and especially religious leaders, has become much more respectable than it used to be. While Freud was alive any *rapprochement* between psychoanalytical thought and organized religion was almost impossible, for he was a nonbeliever and considered religious practice to be a form of neurosis. But analysts today are at least far more temperate in their views and are often ardently religious themselves. Indeed one might almost say that the type of human behavior generally advocated by today's analysts constitutes a revival of such often forgotten basic Christian principles as complete honesty, humility, living by the Golden Rule and the turning of the other cheek.

The churches have tried to meet the psychologists and psychoanalysts half way. About half of all Protestant theological seminaries offer courses in pastoral counseling. An interdenominational Council for Clinical Training, with 43 centers throughout the U. S., provides student and practicing clergymen with actual clinical experience among inmates of mental hospitals, reformatories and prisons. A magazine called *Pastoral Psychology* has 16,000 subscribers, of whom about 14,000 are ministers. And a number of clergymen prominent in the pastoral counseling movement have been psychoanalyzed themselves, the better to understand the work.

Among Jews, the great champion of psychoanalysis was the late Rabbi Joshua Liebman, who learned about it by being successfully analyzed himself, then wrote *Peace of Mind,* which was the publishing sensation of 1946 and eventually sold 900,000 copies. Rabbi Liebman stated flatly that religion needed the help of psychology to make men live by religious ideals, and that "a prepsychological religion cannot satisfy mankind in its quest for salvation in this psychological age." Rabbi Liebman belonged to the liberal or Reform wing of Judaism, whose rabbinical students today must take at least one course in human relations including work in pastoral psychiatry. Conservative rabbis are trained at New York's Jewish Theological Seminary where a board of five psychoanalysts conducts a course in pastoral psychiatry. For all rabbis, Reform, Conservative or Orthodox, the Jewish equivalent of Protestantism's Council for Clinical Training is the Institute for Pastoral Psychiatry which operates at Bellevue Hospital in New York City.

Many Catholic churchmen have vigorously opposed

psychoanalysis in the past but today this attitude seems to be on the wane. A general impression that the practice of psychoanalysis might be sinful *per se* was dispelled by Pope Pius in a 1953 pronouncement which gave official approval to analysis as well as other forms of psychotherapy so long as they are practiced in accordance with Christian principle, that is, with recognition of the existence of the human soul and of the need to abide by the moral precepts of the Church. About a half dozen priests in the United States and Canada have become psychiatrists; one of them is on the staff of a mental hospital in New York City and another runs two psychiatric clinics in Canada. More than a hundred priests belong to the American Catholic Psychological Association, whose membership requirement is a master's degree or better in psychology. A number of Catholic laymen are practicing analysts, and presumably the number will increase as the import of the Pope's words in 1953 takes effect.

All in all the number of those trained and working in the field of psychology and psychiatry is leaping ahead almost by geometrical progression. Many experts think that our present 16,000 psychologists will grow to more than 30,000 in the next 15 years, our present 10,000 psychiatrists (including psychoanalysts) to perhaps 17,000 or even more. All indications are that the expansion of psychology and psychiatry up to now—as spectacular as it has been—is only the beginning.

CHAPTER TWO

Basic Psychology: How We See, Hear and Learn

EVER since the time of Democritus, about 2,400 years ago, wise men have argued over how people see, hear, feel and taste. Democritus came pretty close to guessing the truth, for it was his theory that all objects must give off some kind of invisible substance which penetrates our pores and impinges itself upon our brains. But Democritus and all the philosophers who followed him, up to the time of our present scientific age, really had no way of knowing whether they were right or wrong. Their method was to sit around and speculate. The trees and brooks that we see—are they actually there or are they just an illusion, something that we imagine? Does the world look alike to any two people? If a tree (granted that there is such a thing as a tree) falls where no one is around to hear it, does it make a sound? These questions were debated for centuries without a verdict, each philosopher being free to spin his own answers and argue them to his heart's content.

When the first modern scientific psychologists set up shop around a hundred years ago, it was only natural that they too should have been interested in the age-old mystery of how man gets his impressions of the outside world. "Sensory psychology," as it came to be called, was one of the first big fields of inquiry, and still remains one of their basic tools of knowledge. Along with the subject of learning, sensory psychology makes up a large part of the standard Psychology I course in every college—the primary step in understanding what the age of psychology and psychiatry is all about.

The sensory psychologists broke away sharply from their ancient predecessors by going into the laboratory to look at the facts. There was, for example, the question of how the sense of taste operates. Instead of trying to catalogue all the flavors we seem to taste, from apricot nectar to garlic, they decided to find out experimentally just how sensitive the human tongue is. It developed that the nerve endings in the taste buds, which are in the little bumps that make the tongue rough, are really not very sensitive at all. They can distinguish only four flavors—those which we call sweet, sour, bitter and salty. Most of what we think of as taste was found to be a matter of smell, which accounts for the fact that food seems so tasteless when we are stuffed up with a bad cold.

As for the sense of smell, the psychologists went about the measurements in a manner which serves as a good example of their techniques. They knew from the physiologists that the nerve endings sensitive to odors lie far up in the nasal cavities, at a level just below the eyes. To detect a very mild odor, we have to take a deliberate sniff. But how much is a sniff, and how can any two people be taught to sniff exactly the same amount? To keep their measurements accurate psychologists have used a pressure bottle equipped with nose pieces like a double-barreled atomizer, with which they can blast up against the smelling or olfactory nerves a known amount of vapor containing a known concentration of the substance under test. Or they have dressed their subjects in odorless fabrics and put them into a sealed glass room in which the concentration of the substance can be rigidly controlled. This is the essential difference between modern psychology and mankind's earlier attempts to understand himself by sitting quietly under a tree and examining his thoughts.

We know now—from the psychologists, the physiologists and the physicists—that all our senses depend upon nerve endings which respond to an actual physical stimulus from the world outside. The stimulus can be sound, light or heat waves traveling through the air or an actual molecule of some volatile substance touching our nerves of smell. One attribute of the senses is their amazing efficiency. The psychologists have found, for example, that our noses can detect a substance like artificial musk, a perfume base, in dilutions as fantastically low as one part musk to 32,250 million parts of air. Our eyes can distinguish perhaps as many as a million different hues, shades and intensities of color. Moreover they can adapt themselves so completely to the dark, becoming so sensitive to the tiniest amount of light, that on a clear black night they can see a match struck fifty miles away.

Over and above its great sensitivity and power of discrimination the human eye demonstrates a principle of sensory psychology which is even more important and impressive. The eye has a lens, as every schoolboy now knows, which works like a camera lens. And, as everyone who has ever used a camera with a ground glass back knows, the camera lens turns images upside down and left side to right. Thus our eyes get an upside-down and turned-around picture—but this inverted position of the image does not confuse us; we still see things as right side up (or at least as what the world has come to accept as right side up, though some old-fashioned philosophers might still like to argue). The human senses have a good deal more than mere physical efficiency; they operate in a way which, so to speak, "makes sense." Our impressions of the outside world are right side up; they hang together and form meaningful patterns.

When we are walking along the street, every image that comes to our eyes actually moves across our retinas, since the retinas themselves are moving. But we do not see the sidewalks and store buildings as changing position; we see them as we have come to know them. On the other hand if we are in a train and can see nothing but another train which is moving while we are standing still, we think that we are doing the moving because that is what usually happens in a train. Often, because of the angle, the image of a rectangular door falls on the retina as sloping and distorted; we still see the door as a rectangle. When we first saw a television screen, we were aware that the images there were distorted—people are sometimes made squatter than in real life, and straight lines made wavy— but soon they began to look perfectly natural. We would now have to get out a ruler to convince ourselves that the images are off kilter.

Another example of how our sensory impressions are affected by the sum total of what we know is this psychology experiment: Have someone cut out several newspaper or magazine headlines, all of the same size type. Have him walk away, holding up a headline from time to time, until he is just past the farthest point at which you can read the type. Each time he shows you a headline, he must immediately discard it, so that your knowledge of what it says will not influence you. When he is finally past your range of vision and has shown you a headline which you cannot make out, have him read the headline to you and then show it to you again. You will find that you can now read it—and you will wonder why you could possibly have had any trouble before. A similar phenomenon, but in reverse, often happens in everyday life. We see a face at a distance and are sure it is a friend; we can actually "see" him. But when we get closer we see it is someone entirely different. Or we definitely "see" a dog lying dead on the highway ahead—only to find as we get closer that it is nothing but a piece of old cloth. In these cases our eyes are tricking us, but only in their constant effort to "make sense" out of the images that fall on them.

Psychologists have had a lot of fun with a gadget called a pseudophone, a set of earphones designed so that sounds which would normally enter the left ear are routed over to the right ear, and vice versa. Since our ability to tell what direction a sound is coming from depends on which ear the sound waves strike first, one would think that the pseudophone would give us a completely false sense of direction. And so it does for a time; a car moves past from left to right while its sound goes from right to left. But after a short time of wearing a pseudophone, it loses its ability to fool us; somehow our sensory apparatus adjusts to it. Psychologists have also experimented with spectacle lenses that reverse the rays entering our eyes, so that images now fall right side up on the retina, instead of upside down and left to right. A person wearing these spectacles is terribly confused at first and has a hard time to keep from bumping into chairs and walls or falling downstairs. After a few days, however, the world begins to straighten out and he can automatically move in the right direction, even though he never does get to the point of seeing things right side up through the glasses.

To be sure, our senses are by no means perfect. Our eyes can see only a part of the full range of the wave lengths of light; we have photographic papers, for example, which can take pictures by infrared light which our eyes cannot see at all. Our ears do not hear all sounds;

dogs will respond to "silent whistles" that give forth a sound of too high pitch for the human ear to detect. Many fishes, having taste buds all over their bodies, have a far better sense of taste. In ultimate terms, all our senses are perhaps defective in that they are not keen enough to detect the real nature of matter. We see and feel a solid table, though we know from the physicists that the table is really made up of tiny electrons in constant motion, with gaps of space between them. For all practical purposes, however, our senses do quite a marvelous job of telling us what we need to know. This is the ultimate conclusion of the psychologists, most of whom have now moved on to other fields.

Learning was another of the early interests of the psychologists—and it remains so to this day, for it has been found to be the key process in human behavior. Human beings, unlike many lower creatures, are born without the instincts or built-in nervous patterns which somehow make salmon migrate upstream to spawn and enable robins to build the typical nests and sing the typical song of their species even if they have never seen another robin since birth. The human baby is practically a blank sheet of paper. He knows how to suck and to cry and seems to have an inborn fear of loud noises or falling. But practically everything else in his life must be learned. Even the things we call personality or emotional traits—the fact that one person likes opera while another likes rock 'n' roll, that one is gentle and another hot-tempered, that one likes to be alone while another prefers constant company—all these things seem to be the results of very complicated learning processes. To the psychologist, learning and living are practically synonymous.

The first great experimenter in learning was the Russian psychologist Pavlov, who established the now famous principle of the conditioned reflex. When food is placed in a dog's mouth, the dog salivates—this is a reflex which just naturally happens without the dog's even thinking about it. Pavlov found that if he sounded a bell each time just before he gave a dog food, eventually the bell itself would start salivation. The dog had learned, so to speak, to salivate to the sound of the bell—or, more properly, the salivary reflex had been "conditioned" to the sound of the bell.

Pavlov found in fact that the dog would salivate not only to the sound of a bell but also to similar sounds, such as a buzzer. Thus he established the principle of "stimulus generalization"—the fact that if we respond to a certain stimulus, we will have a similar response to others which are more or less like it. A good many of our unexplained feelings and fears as adults were probably established in this very way in our childhoods. The classic example in psychological literature is the case of Albert, an eleven-month-old boy, and the white rat. At first Albert, when shown the rat, seemed to like it and tried to play with it. Then, every time he was shown the rat, a loud and frightening noise was sounded. Soon Albert was afraid of the rat—he had been "conditioned" to fear it. And it developed that he also showed fear when he saw a white rabbit or even a man with a white beard—his fear response was "generalized" to these objects. The psychologists feel that all the well-known adult phobias may be nothing more than "generalized" responses to a childhood experience—acrophobia (fear of high places) may result from an infant's fall from a chair, claustrophobia (fear of enclosed places) from being punished by being locked in a closet. A child who has come to fear its father because of severe punishment may forever thereafter fear all men who look like him, or indeed all men regardless of appearance, or in fact all people regardless of sex. The Caspar Milquetoast is a man who has "generalized" his fear of someone— probably his father, possibly his mother—to all of humanity.

For a time Pavlov's experiments led many psychologists to take a highly mechanistic view of humanity. Many of the more radical members of the so-called behaviorist school of psychology which had much influence around 1920 believed that there was nothing to human life except one conditioned reflex or response after another, each set off inevitably by the one before it and leading inevitably to the next. John Watson, the leader of the behaviorists, once said that he could take any dozen healthy babies and by training their reflexes turn them into whatever he pleased —doctor, lawyer, beggar or thief.

But psychologists have since established that the conditioned reflex is only one form of learning, and by no means the most common kind at that. We learn by trial and error —as a rat learns to take the right path through a maze to find food. We human beings and a few animals also learn by insight. We look at a problem, think about it and finally solve it—just as the chimpanzee in a famous experiment by psychologist Wolfgang Köhler finally solved the problem of the banana and the two sticks. In this experiment a chimpanzee in a cage had a stick which was not quite long enough to reach a banana which lay outside the cage. Within range of the short stick, however, there also lay outside the cage another stick long enough to reach the banana. After staring at the two sticks and the banana long enough, the chimpanzee finally got the idea; the banana was his, and exploded forever was mankind's self-flattering theory that only man himself can think.

In the course of seeking facts about learning, the psychologists have conducted a number of remarkable experiments with animals even lower in intelligence than dogs and apes. They have been able, for example, to teach the lowly minnow to do a most clever and useful job as a detective in search of polluted water. Like many fishes, minnows have a superb sense of taste and are aware of the tiniest amount of pollution in water. But how could they be used to report it? A psychologist solved this problem with a course of training in which minnows were given an electric shock every time they got near any trace of pollution and thus learned to dart away in great fright. Then when a sample of water to be tested was poured into their tank, they remained calm if it was pure and went into a frenzy if it was polluted.

Cockroaches have been trained to take the right path through a simple maze, and have incidentally shown that in many ways they learn and forget much like human beings. Even the paramecium, a one-celled animal found in

30

stagnant water, has been found capable of a rudimentary type of learning. A psychologist once put a paramecium in a drop of water half of which was dark and half of which was in the light. The drop was ingeniously heated so that the dark half was at normal temperature for the paramecium and the light half was too hot. The paramecium "learned" to avoid the light and did so afterward regardless of temperatures.

The psychologists have also done a great deal of research on how human beings learn all kinds of skills under all kinds of conditions. And from all these experiments, animal and human, have come certain principles of learning which are most helpful to anyone who must acquire new knowledge or skills. The principles of learning have also had a great effect on our schools, notably in demolishing the old notion of "transfer" which once dominated education. It used to be thought that teaching Latin and Greek in some way exercised, trained and disciplined the mind so that it would then be prepared to learn other matters much more readily. But psychologists have proved that learning these things is helpful only in learning similar subjects such as other languages which have a lot of Latin or Greek roots. Otherwise Latin and Greek have no effect on the student's learning ability except insofar as he acquires good study habits and a good attitude toward his work, which he can pick up just as easily while studying something else. It is actually easier to go right ahead and learn French than to spend a lot of time learning Latin first. And mathematical skills, though of course most useful to learn in this period of engineering, show so little "transfer" that students who have never taken algebra can pick up geometry just as fast as those who have.

In some learning situations transfer not only fails to help but actually hinders. An example of "negative transfer," as the psychologists call this, would be an automobile driver changing from a car with standard gearshift to one with automatic transmission; he has to learn *not* to use a clutch and *not* to shift in the old way at the same time he is learning the new methods. Negative transfer is especially bothersome to older people, who find great difficulty at times in abandoning habitual ways of doing things. It is also a potential cause of accidents. The psychologists say that airplane designers, for example, should never bring out new controls which work exactly the opposite way from those the pilots are already used to—lest some pilot revert to old habit in a moment of stress. The same principle applies to the learning of some athletic skills. It is foolish to try to learn to hit a baseball by hitting it just a few feet, for such muscle movements are quite different from those used in a full and free swing and can only interfere. In all probability the same is true of golf, and Ben Hogan is a better psychologist than he realizes when he urges pupils to try to slam the ball as far as they can right from the very start.

The best way to learn practically anything, the psychologists have found, is to take fairly short practice periods, with rest periods between. In learning from the printed page, a combination of reading and trying to recite the material out loud is far better than reading alone. In fact

32

if the study period is one hour, it is better to read for only twelve minutes and recite for forty-eight minutes than to read the entire time—though the best proportion of all is probably about half and half. Learning comes easiest of all when it is what the psychologists call "strongly motivated" —in other words, when we want to learn badly—and one of the best ways of maintaining a strong motivation is to keep track of one's progress. (Golf is again a pretty good example. Golfers, who are always comparing their score with par, usually keep at the game as long as they can walk. Tennis players, who have no such direct way of measuring their day-to-day performance, tend to give up much sooner.) Punishment, on the other hand, seems to have less effect on learning than one might expect. Psychologists have become very skeptical of even the old-fashioned tongue-lashing, by parent, teacher or boss, as an effective incentive to better performance at anything.

In many varieties of learning, as for example in typing, telegraphy, speaking a foreign language or playing a musical instrument, the beginner often makes rapid progress for a time and then seems to have reached his peak. No matter how hard he tries, he does not seem to show any further improvement at all. The psychologists have found that the important thing about this period of more or less standing still, which they call a learning plateau, is that sooner or later it gives way to another period of pronounced progress. The learner who reaches a plateau need not despair, for if he keeps on practicing he will eventually start to improve again. The causes of learning plateaus are not completely understood, but they probably have something to do with establishing new working methods. The typist may at first be thinking of every letter by itself, and soon reach his peak of speed to the point where no further improvement is possible under these conditions. But eventually, as he persists in his practice, he suddenly comes to think in terms of whole words or phrases, and this new method enables him to start making progress once again.

One special field of learning in which the psychologists have some good advice to offer is reading. Many otherwise bright people, from high school students on up, have been found to read very slowly and sometimes almost painfully. The psychologists have discovered their eye movements are the key to their problem. Usually without knowing it, fast readers have trained their eyes to take in a span of as much as two words and sometimes more at a single glance; in moving from left to right on a line the width of this one, their eyes will stop only five or six times. Slow readers, on the other hand, have fallen into the habit of pausing at every single word or in extreme cases at every syllable of every word; on a line like this their eyes may stop as many as twenty times.

It has been discovered, fortunately, that most slow readers can easily reduce their eye movements. The prescription is this: Have someone time you for one minute while you read a very easy book or magazine article as fast as you possibly can without losing complete track of what it says. To make sure you are not losing track, have your timer quiz you on what you have read. Count how many words you read during the minute. The next day do this again, always trying for speed and more speed. Many people who try this find that within a few weeks they can read twice as many words per minute as when they started, and actually remember the words better.

Although nobody can say exactly what goes on in our nervous systems when we are learning, the most logical and generally accepted theory is that the process has something to do with the structures called synapses, the connections where one nerve fiber ends and another begins. Here the impulse from the first nerve must leap a gap, so to speak, and set off an impulse in the second nerve. Many synapses are multiple connections where the impulse can go in one or more directions. In fact the brain itself is a mass of synapses, like a giant telephone switchboard. Once certain connections have been made at the synapses, the psychologists believe, it becomes easier for nerve impulses to take the same path again.

It used to be thought that forgetting was simply a matter of the paths eventually fading out if never used again. But subsequent studies have shown that the paths never do seem to fade away completely. In charting how much we forget and how quickly, the psychologists have established that there is a standard curve of forgetting which seems to apply to almost any knowledge which is not used or practiced for a time.

The curve is quite steep at first and then flattens out. Suppose that a woman studies French in college, then never speaks or reads French again. After six months she may have forgotten half of what she knew, after a year three-fourths of it, after two years perhaps 90 per cent. But the 10 per cent that she then remembers will diminish very slowly in succeeding years, and she will probably always remember some of it. In fact she will discover, if the occasion ever demands, that her college French has made a greater impression on her than she ever realized. If she begins studying French again, even twenty or thirty years later, she will find herself quickly passing the students who are studying it for the first time. In this sense of helping us to relearn, nothing that we learn is ever really forgotten.

The new theory of forgetting is that each of our memories is obscured and sometimes nearly obliterated by interference from all our other thoughts and experiences. Our minds, so to speak, are like a blackboard used over and over again without erasing anything. The child starts out with a clean board, and everything written upon it stands out clear, bold and easily remembered. But as we grow up—particularly in our complicated modern world, and with our lengthened span of life—we do so many things, we learn so much, we absorb so many impressions, that we begin to have a hard time keeping things straight. We keep writing on the blackboard, and everything new is all mixed up with everything that was there before it and everything that will be written afterward. Everything we try to remember is obscured by everything we learned before (what the psychologists call proactive inhibition) and by everything we did afterward (retroactive inhibition).

Most of us feel, as we get older, that we become increasingly forgetful and absent-minded. This seems to be largely a matter of having put so much writing on the blackboard that proactive and retroactive inhibition now work overtime. Actually studies have shown that our learning ability reaches its peak in the mid-twenties, then declines thereafter at an extremely slow rate. A fifty-year-old man, for all his worries about his bad "memory," can learn things just as fast as the fifteen-year-old son or daughter who seems so bright and alert. After fifty, to be sure, the decline is more rapid.

In their studies of learning and forgetting the psychologists have come upon the answer to another question which, like the old problem of how people see and hear, was the subject of considerable speculation for centuries. This is the question of whether people are born equal and would all turn out alike if they had the same opportunities. The psychologists quickly proved that people differ quite markedly in their ability to learn and to remember what they have learned—and presumably do so from birth. Nor is there any consolation for poor learners in the fact that they are slow. Contrary to what used to be the accepted notion, it is the quick, effortless learner, not the laborious plodder, who best remembers what he has studied.

The intelligence test, a measure of the ability to learn, is perhaps the best-known invention of the psychologist. The first one was developed by a French psychologist named Binet in 1905, at the request of school authorities who wanted to weed out children who could not possibly profit from instruction. Since then various individual and group tests have been perfected and the initials I.Q.—intelligence quotient—have become a household phrase, though perhaps not everyone understands quite what the term means. It is a sort of index number of intelligence, based on mental development as compared to actual age.

A figure of 100 indicates average intelligence. If a child of five gets as high a score on an intelligence test as the average child of seven he has an I.Q. of 140. If he does only as well as the average child of four, he has an I.Q. of only 80. When this child who scored 80 is ten years old, he will do only as well as the average child of eight, for the I.Q. remains constant as we grow up.

In giving intelligence tests to hundreds of thousands of people, the psychologists have pretty well established that intellectual capacity is inherited. Like all other inheritable traits, it may come from distant ancestors rather than from the immediate parents, so that college professors sometimes have dull sons and stupid parents sometimes have brilliant children, or the same family may have one bright, one average and one dull child. Nonetheless it works out by and large that brighter parents tend to have brighter children. The children of professional men have been shown to have the highest I.Q.s (averaging around 115) and those of day laborers the lowest (around 96). A child born into a poor home often shows an improvement in I.Q. if adopted by a more intelligent and stimulating family, and it has been found that Negro children born into backward rural families improve steadily if they move to the city. But the amount of improvement is always limited by the mental capacity that was there at birth.

Although intelligence tests are occasionally given too much weight, they have been a boon to educators, for they tell a lot about students and the way they are getting along. In a second-grade classroom, for example, there may be two boys who consistently fail to get their work done. In the old days these two boys would have been lumped together as disciplinary problems. Nowadays the teacher may find that one boy is below normal in intelligence and unable to keep up even though trying his best, whereas the other has superior intelligence and simply cannot get interested in work at the second-grade level. The tests are also useful as rough guides to vocational placement for adults. It has been found, for example, that half of all accountants have I.Q.s of 125 or higher, and that few successful accountants score below 110. Thus a young man whose I.Q. is under 110 should think twice before choosing accounting as a profession, and he should be prepared to find himself at a considerable disadvantage unless it is much higher. On the other hand farm workers and miners have an average I.Q. of about 90, and some people are working successfully and happily at these jobs with I.Q.s of 70 or less.

How many smart people are there in the United States, and how many dull ones? Most of us are right around the average; indeed 46 per cent of us score between 90 and 109. Going up or down the scale from this point, the numbers drop off rapidly:

140 and up	Very superior	1%
120–139	Superior	11%
110–119	High average	18%
90–109	Average	46%
80–89	Low average	15%
70–79	Borderline	6%
Below 70	Mental defective	3%

The 1 per cent who score above 140 are the geniuses and near-geniuses. Contrary to old-fashioned opinion they are on the whole healthier and more stable than the average person. They do not burn out young and they enjoy unusual success as adults, though their exceptional ability to learn quickly does sometimes cause problems of school and social adjustment. The 3 per cent who score below 70 are the morons (I.Q. of 50–69), imbeciles (20–49) and idiots (below 20) of our world. Some of them get along fairly well despite their mental limitations, for a moron who learns the social graces and the virtue of not talking too much can achieve quite a reputation as a sportsman or a housewife-hostess, and even imbeciles can sometimes be taught to be self-supporting after a fashion. But in general those with I.Q.s below 70 constitute a grave social problem and a very large one—for 3 per cent amounts to over 5 million people in the United States.

A psychologist once tried a most provocative experiment with animals in selective breeding for intelligence. Starting with a group of 142 white rats chosen at random, he picked out the smartest and dullest ones, as determined by their ability to learn a path through a maze. The bright ones were then mated within their own group, as were the dull ones. In the resulting new generation, the psychologist again picked out the brightest and dullest for further mating. After seven generations he had two remarkably dissimilar groups, one group averaging very smart and the other averaging very dull. Later he permitted the two groups to interbreed, as in nature. The next generation was just about like the group with which he had started—a few very bright, a few very dull and the great majority in-between.

Doubtless this experiment has some theoretical implications for the human race, but it hardly promises us a breed of super-geniuses for tomorrow. Even the once popular notion of eliminating feeble-mindedness by sterilizing all feeble-minded people has been proved impracticable. It has been estimated that even after sterilizing 68 generations of the feeble-minded, a project that would take until somewhere around the year 4000, the world would still have a good many feeble-minded people, perhaps actually a tenth as many as today. One of the most important things the psychologists have learned about intelligence, in the last analysis, is that you can't do much about it.

CHAPTER THREE

Psychology in Industry, School and Everyday Life

WHEN psychologists were developing their basic principles through laboratory experiments in perception and learning, they never suspected how popular they were about to become. Certainly they never expected to be embraced by the business world. The old-fashioned businessman, after all, had strong notions of his own about humanity. To hire a man, who needed anything more than common sense? Any businessman could look at an applicant, talk to him and tell right away if he was a good worker. Training? You simply put him under a good tough foreman and if he had the stuff he would learn the job; if not you fired him. Hours? The longer the better; anybody knows you can do more work in sixty hours than fifty. Morale? There's nothing that a raise won't cure.

It all made good common sense. But when a few pioneer psychologists left the classroom a generation or so ago to study these truisms, they turned out to be mostly untrue. One famous early experiment, conducted in 1916, was directed at learning how well a group of businessmen could judge job applicants in the traditional face-to-face meeting. The interviewers were twenty-three experienced men, mostly sales managers who hired salesmen all the time. Each of them individually talked to and rated the same twenty-four applicants. The results were almost as helter-skelter as if the names had been written on sheets of paper and churned up by an electric fan. No single applicant was ranked first by more than three of the twenty-three interviewers. One man was ranked first by one interviewer—but sixteenth, nineteenth and twenty-second by others.

A sociologist, first cousin to the psychologists, tried another experiment and pretty well found out what is wrong with the interview method. He assigned twelve people to interview 2,000 homeless men and try to find out what had put them on the skids. Among the interviewers were an ardent Prohibitionist and a confirmed Socialist. The Prohibitionist found that the chief cause of the men's downfall was drink. The Socialist found that the chief cause was capitalism. The moral was that no interviewer can really see beyond the end of his own prejudices.

Out of such experiments has been born the subscience called industrial psychology, which more modern businessmen are heeding all the time. Indeed the application of laboratory knowledge to practical problems, in business and elsewhere, is rapidly becoming the psychologist's chief occupation. A few decades ago psychology's leaders were wondering where jobs could be found for all the students who had become interested in the subject. Now their worry is quite the opposite. With so many young psychologists streaming off the campus to take well-paid work in industry or government, the problem is whether the science is being frozen at too low a level of knowledge for lack of sufficient people doing pure research.

Perhaps the best-known application of psychology in our daily lives is the test—not just the intelligence test described in the previous chapter, but the test for practically everything the human body can perform or the mind conceive. There are individual tests and group tests, written tests and oral tests; many are of proven value and some may turn out to be utterly absurd. There are tests for physical skills like manual dexterity and finger dexterity, for such talents as mechanical aptitude and musical aptitude, for personality traits like introversion, extroversion, masculinity and femininity. The manufacture, printing, sale and administration of tests is a multimillion-dollar business. Business firms use them to select the people they will hire and the people who will get promotions. The military services use them to decide which men will become aircraft pilots, radar operators, mechanics or typist-clerks. Colleges and private consulting firms use them to tell young people which careers to attempt.

Test scores are graded and calibrated according to the techniques of psychological statistics, an adaption of some of the mathematician's tools. The person who takes them is usually ranked on what is called a percentile scale—a score of 75 meaning that he is better than 74.9 per cent of those who have taken the test but not so good as the other 25 per cent, a score of 50 meaning that he stands in the middle, and a score of one putting him at the very bottom. This has led some critics to deplore psychological tests as an attempt to reduce all human affairs to a bleak and mechanical rating system. Others have called the tests an unwarranted intrusion on private lives. But actually even the old-fashioned interview was a test of a kind in which the applicant had to live up to the interviewer's notions of how an applicant should talk. So was the trial period which used to be a standard practice. The only thing different about the psychological tests is that they attempt to establish ratings in an accurate and scientific fashion.

A study of people who had selected their careers on the basis of psychologically sound vocational guidance, based mainly on tests, once showed that twenty-eight had succeeded for every one person who failed. For a similar group not given guidance, the ratio of success to failure was only 50–50. The Army's results are perhaps even more spectacular. It first gives a general intelligence test to its recruits, and the lowest 10 per cent are immediately eliminated as untrainable. It then gives tests for aptitude in radio code, maintenance work, technical jobs, combat and other military tasks. By gearing actual training and assignment to these tests the Army finds it can take the average recruit and get as much efficiency from him as if he had scored twenty percentage points higher in the intelligence test. Thus the tests have been proved to work. That is, the good ones work, when properly used. Unfortunately, the process has become such a fad that a good many phony tests have managed to sneak in undetected; many of those now in general use are about as useful, in the words of one psychologist, "as a rubber yardstick."

The creation of a good, accurate, reliable test of any human ability is an extremely lengthy and difficult process. Suppose, for example, that one is seeking a test for truck drivers, as the Army actually did over a five-year period. The first thing is to evaluate the standard state drivers' license tests, which most recruits have already passed. (Usually these tests prove very little except that the applicant is breathing and not blind.) The next thing is to try to discover what makes a good truck driver—how the good ones differ from the bad ones in physical characteristics, temperament, reaction time and various types of knowledge, dexterity and skill, as well as in many matters of personal life and habit. Once it is decided what characteristics seem to make a good truck driver, the test then has to be designed to try to measure these things. Finally it must be administered to thousands of people to find out what constitutes a good or a bad score, and these people have to be followed up to see if the test actually separates the successes from the failures. All this takes a lot of time and money, which have to be invested without guarantee of success. After much work Army psychologists finally came up with a test for truck drivers which seems to be pretty accurate—but they might just as easily have failed.

A lot of jerry-built psychological tests in wide use today have never themselves been tested—or as the psychologist says, "validated"—in this careful fashion. They represent only one man's opinion of what a good test might be and have no more actual scientific value than did the old-fashioned businessman's snap judgments based on common sense. In this class fall most of the tests used inside companies for the selection of executives. Since nobody has ever proved scientifically what it is that makes a good executive—and since the qualities expected of an executive probably vary widely from industry to industry and company to company—how in the world can anybody expect to draw up a test? Even the good tests, moreover, are frequently misused by overenthusiastic customers. Some company presidents and personnel men have become so intrigued by the idea that they can spot the brightest people in a group of applicants that they refuse to hire any others—and have made grievous mistakes by assigning extremely quick-witted and easily bored people to run elevators, or city slickers with a large and high-flown vocabulary to sell hog feed to sharecroppers. The tests are really useful only when used as they are supposed to be used by trained psychologists—and the more modest psychologists at that. Some of the psychologists who have gone into industry and succumbed to the lure of quick results and a quick dollar are the object of much head-shaking by their more conservative colleagues.

Inside the office and factory the psychologists have discovered a number of interesting and useful things. They have learned, above all, that fatigue plays a much greater part in the work day than the old-time businessman ever realized. Practically every worker, physical or mental, is at his peak early in the day, as soon as he has got warmed up to the job, and falls off fairly rapidly thereafter, until he is accomplishing practically nothing at all at the end of the day. Even in wartime or other emergency it does no good to increase the work week past fifty-four hours, because that is just about the absolute limit of human capacity—and a worker will get as much done in fifty-four hours as he will in sixty or seventy. Decreasing the work week from fifty-four hours to forty, which is a matter of 26 per cent, does not decrease output anywhere near that much, for a week of about forty hours is just about ideal from the standpoint of efficiency per hour.

Rest periods are a great help to efficiency; the worker who loafs now and again gets more done than the one who tries to keep going all the time. In one experiment girls on a labeling job raised their production 13 per cent when given a ten-minute rest period in the middle of the morning. Girls assembling bicycle chains increased production—also, as it happened, by 13 per cent—as a result of five-minute rest periods at the end of each hour. On more strenuous tasks, even more rest seems to be ideal; one psychologist has figured that a man doing light muscular work on an eight-hour shift must rest just about one-sixth of the time to be at peak efficiency. Industrial psychologists nowadays advise employers to provide rest periods as a standard and authorized part of the work day. It has been found that workers will take them anyway, at the water cooler or in the rest room, and that authorized ones are much more effective.

The most important factor of all when it comes to increasing production, however, seems to be worker morale, a subject which has occupied the industrial psychologist's close attention ever since a famous experiment at the Western Electric Company in 1927. This started as a simple matter of illumination engineering; the company merely wanted to learn how much light would bring about maximum production in various departments where girls assembled telephone apparatus. But it was immediately discovered, to everyone's surprise, that as soon as the company began experimenting with the lights, production went up regardless of whether the wattage was increased or decreased. It even went up when an electrician pretended to change all the bulbs in a room but put the same ones back. Something strange was at work and the company spent the next five years trying to discover just what.

The company tried giving the girls rest periods, different hours, a shorter week. Production kept going up. Then all the new privileges were taken away. Production went up again. Finally there was only one possible conclusion: the girls working in the plant were responding to the attention being paid them, not to any specific form that the attention took from day to day. They thought the company was interested in them, they felt important and they worked harder. Their improved morale was more vital to production than all the physical aspects of their working conditions put together.

In contrast to the girls at Western Electric, men at the same plant were found to be less emotional about their jobs and far more concerned about practical matters. Even among men, however, numerous studies have shown that pay alone is not the crucial factor. Nor can a company "buy" loyalty through such devices as improving the cafeteria meals or running bowling contests, which have been tried and found ineffective. What counts most seems to be the warmth or coldness of the worker's relations with his foreman or supervisor and the amount of respect each has for the other. The attempt to teach supervisors how best to work with their employees has become a big part of the industrial psychologist's job.

Psychologists have known for a long time that one of the greatest problems in business and industry is the disturbed worker—the man or woman who is in such bad shape emotionally that happiness and efficiency on the job are almost impossible. A pioneer study at a Connecticut silk mill showed that mental and emotional disturbances caused more loss of time and money than all contagious diseases and accidents put together. Another early study of 4,000 people who had been fired from their jobs showed that nearly two thirds failed for reasons of social incompetence—poor relations with their fellow workers or bosses —rather than actual inability to do the job.

More recently a large statistical study of telephone operators disclosed that a mere third of them—all of whom had personal problems of one kind or another—were responsible for the bulk of all the absenteeism, illness and accidents. Other studies have indicated that in fact perhaps as many as 80 per cent or 90 per cent of all industrial accidents are due to human error of one kind or another, the bulk of them committed by workers who seem to have one mishap after another and are sometimes said by psychologists to be "accident prone." Many such workers show a pattern of having accidents on the same days of the week or at the same hours of the day. On the other hand some psychologists feel that the most difficult worker of all is the one who does not quite have an accident, does not quite get sick enought to stay home—but comes to the job in such a low physical state and such a bad mood that he pulls down the morale and efficiency of everyone around him.

Another problem worker who exists in considerable numbers is the alcoholic or near-alcoholic, who keeps his fellow workers busy covering up for him during his frequent lapses. It has been estimated that about two workers out of 100, or well over a million in all in the United States, fall into this class—and that by far the majority are in the 35–55 age range where industry has a heavy investment in them and they could be at their peak of performance were it not for their drinking.

Some firms, among them du Pont, Metropolitan Life, American Cyanamid and Caterpillar Tractor, have decided to provide employees with the free services of psychiatrists or clinical psychologists. To make their work somewhat more palatable, it is often simply called personnel counseling. Nobody yet knows how successful it is. Certainly it is drastically limited by lack of time and the impossibility of providing enough psychotherapists to undertake intensive treatment of all those who could profit from it.

51

But there have been some indications, as at the Oak Ridge atom bomb plant during the war, that even a very small amount of on-the-job therapy has considerable effect and carries over into the workman's home situation, making him happier all around. It has also been found that providing personnel counseling greatly reduces the work load of foremen and supervisors, who otherwise have to spend much of their time listening to personal problems anyway.

Counseling has its severe critics, however. Many union people refer to it contemptuously as "cow psychology"— an attempt to get more production out of the worker by keeping him placid and uncomplaining. Some psychologists agree, on the ground that any advice paid for by the company is almost bound to favor the company's desires over the worker's psychological needs.

Among those in industry who have been found to have their share of psychological problems are the executives. Perhaps they have even more than their share. The higher up in industry a man goes the more he is likely to worry about his chances of staying there, and the more opportunity he has for that common human failing of comparing himself unfavorably with his colleagues and competitors. To add to the tension, the executive has very few if any intimates to whom he can confide his problems. One executive visited the company psychiatrist out of worry that he was simply outclassed by the brilliant talents of his chief assistant. At the same time the assistant was visiting the psychiatrist out of fear that his own meager talents would never enable him to keep up with the boss.

The services of the psychologist at the executive level

received considerable publicity some months ago from W. Harold Rea, head of Canadian Oil Companies, Ltd., in a speech before Toronto's National Sales Executives Club. Rea told of a company whose president had called in a psychologist to examine all the top men, including the president himself. The psychologist administered a battery of intelligence, aptitude and personality tests and interviewed all the executives in depth. At the end of the study the psychologist reported bluntly that the president was the chief cause of the company's difficulties—he was a worrier and a penny pincher, far too indecisive and unwilling to delegate authority.

After a spell of deep gloom during which he thought of resigning, the president was persuaded to stay on but to redefine the other executives' jobs, give them more authority and let them handle all problems except the big ones that really deserved his attention. As a result the other executives took a renewed interest in their work and the president's desk, cleared of unnecessary details, ceased to be a bottleneck. The company's sales and profits improved sharply. At the end of his speech Rea said, "The company I have been talking about is my own company. The chief executive I have been talking about was your speaker."

Not all company executives who have used the services of psychologists are so frank as Rea, and the results are not always so spectacular. But the use of psychology at the executive level seems on the rise. Several firms of consulting psychologists specialize in this service to the exclusion of all else. At least the psychologist can surely offer the executive more than the standard advice which he used to get from his family doctor—to take a Florida vacation if things became too disagreeable or to ask for a transfer if they became unbearable. The enforced idleness of an unwanted vacation or the added strains of a new job are just about the last thing an already harassed executive can use.

Human engineering, another of the psychologist's contributions to industry, sounds offhand like an attempt by some hardhearted slide-rule expert to remake mankind in a more efficient image. Actually it is just the opposite: an attempt to make machines conform to people. The newest telephone handsets are perhaps the most widely known example. Their design was preceded by measurement of the faces of thousands of people, as well as numerous experiments in which sets of various weights were tried out on users. The new sets which grew out of these observations are lighter than the old ones. They are also shorter, and the mouthpiece is set at an angle which suits the maximum number of people. The dial numbers are outside the holes instead of inside, providing greater legibility and less wear.

All this sounds perfectly simple, but nobody was doing anything like it until recently. Most industrial design has been based on quite different principles—usually on what was easiest to make or what was done by tradition for many years. The home electricity meter with its half dozen little needles moving in different directions on a half dozen little dials is a flagrant example of bad human engineering and is gradually being replaced by a meter which can be read like the mileage on an automobile speedometer. The automobile whose instruments were reflected in the windshield was another human engineering error rampant a few years ago. Most factories and plants are themselves full of bad design: machines with controls in awkward places, work routines that require far too much stooping, bending and walking.

The widest use of human engineering has been made by the armed forces, which learned in World War II that military equipment was getting too complicated and specialized for the men who had to use it. Gun turrets on Navy bombers were far too small for anybody but jockeys, and there was a limited number of jockeys in the draft calls. The Air Force had bomb sights which theoretically could hit a pickle barrel but due to human failure often missed entire cities. The Army had one vehicle which worked just fine except for a seat which vibrated so much that a monkey strapped to it was killed inside three hours.

Much of the early work in human engineering for the military involved such simple steps as changing the shape of aircraft control knobs so that pilots could tell by touch whether they had grasped the landing gear or flap lever. In the last 10 years the work has become increasingly complex and ingenious. Psychologists have now arranged to put many of the important airplane instruments into standard position, with the needles all pointing the same way when the plane is working properly. Better still, the Navy is working on a radically redesigned cockpit system in which practically all the instruments and dials will be replaced by two simple electronic "pictures" that the pilot can read at a glance.

In old-style submarines the controls have been operated

by three men cramped into the tightest of quarters; the controls on the new atom-powered subs can be operated by one man in a comfortable chair. The psychologists are even anticipating maintenance problems and redesigning equipment so that it will be easier to repair as well as to operate. Complicated electronic equipment is now color-coded as it is built, so that repairmen can follow the circuits at a glance.

The psychologists have also undertaken to simplify and improve military training. In some cases they have rede-signed the equipment, as with a shipboard control system which once required four or five weeks of training before its operators were even fair at the job, but now might be handled perfectly by a ten-year-old boy on the first attempt. In other cases they have designed new training equipment which speeds the process. A spectacular example involves the Air Force K-bombing device, which weighs a ton and costs around $250,000. In the past there have never been enough of these expensive devices for the training of repairmen, who have had a very poor record because of lack of practice. Psychologists have built a simple little substitute, costing about $4,000, which gives trainees all the practice they need in finding the possible sources of trouble. Similarly the Army has found that it can use fifty-dollar wooden tank hulls for much of its armored force training instead of tying up several hundred thousand dollars' worth of real tanks. The Air Force has found that its pilots learn just as well when they get their first twenty-five hours of flying instruction in a cheap light plane rather than one costing ten times as much.

The great goal now in training, especially in the Air Force where so many new planes and missiles are coming along, is to have men ready to operate new apparatus before it even comes off the assembly line. The first experiment along this line was made just five years ago when a psychologist was given the specifications and blueprints for a new type of radar equipment. Actually the equipment was already in use, but the psychologist was not told this. With nothing but the plans to work from, he drew up a personnel chart which was substantially in agreement with the actual number of people and types of skill which had been found necessary to keep the equipment in working order. Ever since then the Air Force has assigned about a fifth of all its psychologists to concentrate solely on setting up advance training programs for equipment which will not be received for months and even years. This is the best and perhaps only way, the Air Force figures, to reduce the lag between design and actual use of equipment which makes so much of it obsolete so very fast.

In everyday civilian life one of the most famous applications of psychology is the Gallup poll. Before the science of psychological statistics came along, straw ballots were simply taken at random and with no thought to representative sampling; this led to the old *Literary Digest*'s notorious error in predicting a decisive victory for Landon over Roosevelt in 1936. Now polls like Gallup's are taken with every type of voter represented according to his actual proportion in our society: so many men and so many women, so many farmers and factory workers, so many rich people and poor. Questions are tested in advance to make sure they are not loaded in favor of one response or another. There is still a chance of error but it has been greatly reduced. Not all surveys, of course, are made under best statistical procedure—and it is a good idea to ask how the figures were obtained before believing them.

Polls have been widely used by government—for example to try to determine in the 1930s what kind of crop controls farmers would accept—and especially by business, which uses them to test the popularity of television shows and the reaction to various types of advertising and public relations campaigns. The effectiveness of advertising slogans has been tested in this manner, with results showing that the number of people recognizing the slogan may vary from as little as 1 or 2 per cent for a poor one to 70 per cent for a really good one. Other surveys have shown that face powder sells better in a blue box than a green one, that tan automobiles are more popular in the West than in the East and that a blue-tinted box will sell eggs 30 per cent faster than any other color.

A company once asked a research firm to test public reaction to a shoe preparation it was about to put on the market. The research firm reported that a great many women disliked the can because its border design looked like a worm crawling around; the company put out the product anyway and went broke. Another company spent a small fortune advertising the purity, smoothness and antiseptic properties of its talcum powder—only to find in a survey that 95 per cent of its customers bought it because they liked the smell and the other 5 per cent because they liked the shape of the can.

The newest psychological technique in the advertising field is called "motivational research," or MR for short, and is the subject of much violent argument among both advertisers and psychologists. It has long been known by the psychologists that we often behave as we do for motives completely different from the ones we like to think we have. Dislike of another person's race or religion, to cite a common example, is less often a considered opinion than a process of merely foisting off on someone else our own frustrations and inferiorities. Similarly we perhaps buy new automobiles or bow ties for reasons which are not entirely obvious to us. Some of the motivational research experts in the advertising business claim that they can learn these motives and sell more goods by gearing advertisments to them.

Some of the things the MR experts do seem eminently sensible. One of them advised Pan American-Grace Airways to quit using pictures of pretty models to advertise its South American tours and instead show the kind of middle-aged couples who actually have the money to take such trips. Brewers were advised that they would get nowhere trying to sell their product as a luxury item but should direct their ads to the homey and comfortable people who drink the most beer. The company that makes Marlboro cigarets abandoned its strictly feminine advertising appeal in favor of the tattooed hand it now uses to attract men, who are after all the biggest smokers. Other examples of MR are likely to stagger the imagination. One MR practitioner has come up with the theory that contributing or not contributing to charity is related to the toilet-training period, when the child first discovers that it can please or displease its mother by giving or not giving. Another claims that adolescent girls wash a lot to cleanse themselves of their emerging sex impulses, and that any soap manufacturer who is not ashamed to exploit this hidden motive can get rich.

MR is one of the aspects of psychology which sometimes make it seem like a dark and nefarious science of controlling man's soul and leading him around like any mechanical robot by pushing the right buttons. Another is "psychological warfare," a term much publicized in recent years, with all its frightening implications of a science of persuasion which can lead men to fight or to lay down their arms without a struggle. There is no reason as yet, however, for lovers of mankind's individuality to abandon all hope. MR as an advertising weapon, as has been said, is still an object of much argument among the psychologists themselves, many of whom think it is largely nonsense. As for psychological warfare, this is still mostly a name, and not a very apt one. As one eminent psychologist has pointed out, it resembles the Holy Roman Empire, which was neither holy nor Roman, for it is neither good psychology nor any kind of warfare. What it is, really, is simply old-fashioned propaganda masquerading under a fancy modern name.

The psychologist has found, to be sure, some rather effective ways of appealing to our baser motives and designing propaganda for maximum effect. He has learned the startling fact that even when a piece of literature is presented to students as a horrible example of propaganda, it still often affects their opinions. Propaganda is not, however, a sure key to the control of human beings. One famous study of the 1940 election showed that voters exposed to all kinds of Republican and Democratic propaganda usually chose to believe only what they were already prepared to believe. Any astute observer who knew them at the beginning of the campaign could pretty well have predicted how they would vote, regardless of the pressures brought to bear on them. It was only those voters who were exposed to completely one-sided propaganda who showed any substantial change.

Thus any grave fears that the psychologist may some day betray humanity rest on two assumptions: first, that he will become infinitely better at influencing people than he has proved to date; and second, that all psychologists will gravitate to the side of evil. Neither of these seems very likely at the moment. Doubtless the psychologist will discover many techniques that would be at least moderately dangerous in the wrong hands or if used for the wrong purposes. But competition alone may well save the day. For every advertiser urging us to buy one brand of cigarets there will always be a dozen others attempting to lure us elsewhere. Moreover, the adult human being is infinitely complex and far more impervious to manipulation than we sometimes realize. The psychoanalysts, as we shall see in the next chapter, have found that it often takes years just to understand all the diverse and complicated matters that have influenced our growing up, and that changing our adult personalities is always difficult and sometimes impossible.

CHAPTER FOUR

The ABC of Psychoanalysis

OF ALL the many people engaged in the psychology boom, it is the psychoanalyst who has most thoroughly captured the popular imagination. His very working methods, insofar as the public knows or imagines them, have a fascinating air of the black art about them. His couch, his notebook, his look of intense concentration as he waits to pounce upon a seemingly insignificant remark and use it to unlock the whole secret of the unconscious mind, all make him seem like an exotic, mysterious, half-kindly and half-frightening high priest, privy to secrets beyond the ken of the average man. In a sense he satisfies two of mankind's oldest appetites—for the occult and for the sinful.

The principles on which the psychoanalyst operates have spread their influence far beyond the therapeutic couch. Practically everybody nowadays accepts and acts upon some of the basic concepts of the Freudian psychoanalytic theory—such notions as the unconscious mind, repression, and the lasting role of primitive urges in our adult personalities. Dr. Benjamin Spock's famous book on babies, consulted in some eight million families for advice on such common household medical problems as coughs, colds and rashes, is firmly rooted in Freudian principle. All "motivational research" and all psychological warfare are based on the Freudian notion that many of our actions can be traced to motives and drives that we never suspect. Even those of us who might claim that psychoanalysis is nonsense take it for granted that slips of the tongue, forgotten appointments or a tendency to have one accident after another are a meaningful reflection of our true feelings and personalities, which was one of Freud's great discoveries. It is no exaggeration to state that practically all the work and thinking now being done in the fields of psychology and psychiatry—even by the sharpest critics of Freud—assume in one way or another that at least part of what Freud said was completely correct and vastly important.

Considering the influence of the analysts in our society, some of the statistics about them are quite startling. Freud certainly cast a big pebble into our century's pool of thought —but in terms of the actual number of people involved, the spread of psychoanalysis has been more like the waves in a molasses vat. This is because the training of an analyst is a slow and painful process; each analyst can create only a few others even if he devotes most of his time to teaching. The classic treatment is equally time-consuming. Working a forty-hour week, about all that is humanly possible in such a difficult and demanding profession, an analyst can treat only about ten patients at any given time, seeing each of them three to five times a week. Since each patient is supposed to remain in analysis two to five years, sometimes even longer, the average practitioner fully analyzes no more than 150 patients in his working lifetime. Thus in the entire world today there are only approximately 1,400 practicing psychoanalysts, perhaps 14,000 people undergoing analysis and certainly no more than 100,000 people who have completed analysis. All the living analysts and their past and present patients could be amply accommodated in a single medium-sized city like Scranton, Pennsylvania or Savannah, Georgia.

Because so few people have ever had any intimate experience with the psychoanalyst, a good many myths about him have gained wide acceptance. In the movies, the cartoons and the popular imagination, the analyst tends to look foreign, wear a beard and hold forth in a luxurious penthouse atop an expensive Park Avenue apartment building, where he is titillated all day long by the engrossing details of the sex lives of the nation's most beautiful and wealthy women. Nothing could be further from the truth. In the first place, there is no longer anything "foreign" about psychoanalysis. Almost from the very beginning, Freud's ideas seemed to take hold more quickly in the open-minded United States than in his native Vienna, a city whose stodginess he despised. The westward migration of psychoanalysis was then completed by Hitler, from whom Freud and most of his closest followers, being Jews, fled in the early 1930s. Today the United States is the center of psychoanalysis, and about 50 per cent of all the analysts in the world are native-born Americans. They wear no beards—indeed 15 per cent of them are women and could scarcely be expected to—and in appearance are completely undistinguishable from bankers, teachers, dentists and businessmen. One analyst likes to tell of the time he went to a meeting of analysts at the Waldorf-Astoria Hotel in New York City, wandered into the wrong conference room and was unaware for quite some time that he was attending a convention of plumbing manufacturers by mistake.

Far from being wealthy, most analysts have to watch their budgets just like anybody else. Only the rare analyst can charge fifty dollars an hour; most of them charge twenty. Their income is rigidly limited by the number of hours they can work and often drastically reduced by teaching, lecturing, writing and free clinical service. They do not exactly starve, but on the other hand they do not make as much money on the average as other big-city medical specialists. Nor do they have anywhere near so long a working life as the average man. The education of the analyst is just beginning when he gets his first college degree and watches most of his classmates go off to work. He must then take his M.D., his internship, lengthy analytical training, three years in a psychiatric hospital and his own analysis, for which he pays like anyone else. Ordinarily an analyst is not ready to see his first private patient until he is about thirty-five years old—and heavily in debt for his prolonged education. He is likely to be in his fifties before he has his debts cleared up, a steady practice established and can consider himself independent.

As a matter of fact no analyst can ever really be sure of a steady practice. It is an essential feature of analytic treatment, for reasons which will be explained shortly, that the doctor must be as anonymous, colorless and neutral as possible. He cannot successfully treat any of his relatives or friends, or anyone else with whom he has had any substantial social relations. This means that he can utilize few of the avenues of friendship and social acquaintance by which other doctors commonly enlarge their practices. Moreover his patients are by the very nature of their ailments flighty and unreliable. Wealthy patients—the very ones who can best afford analysis—often are scarcely embarked upon the treatment before they find an excuse to get away on a foreign cruise, or go rushing into a new marriage which makes them feel so much better temporarily that they decide their problems are over. Sometimes patients break off abruptly because of the objections of families who either disbelieve in psychoanalysis, are ashamed of it, or become alarmed by the unavoidable fact that analytic patients often seem to get worse before they get better.

As to what analysts hear all day long, the truth is that human problems tend to be depressingly similar, and often psychoanalysts get the impression that they are listening to the same monotonous phonograph record played over and over again. One of the vexatious problems of the analyst is staying awake at times like this. On the other hand, if his patients are highly disturbed, tense and emotional, he may have to fight to keep his own emotions on an even keel. After a final hour of the working day spent with an overwrought patient reliving a scene of deep grief, the analyst often finds it difficult to go home and take a normal interest in a wife's shopping problems or a son's concern over a broken bicycle.

Although sex plays a key part in Freud's theory of how people become neurotic, it need not necessarily come in for much discussion at all in the day-by-day course of an analysis, which is considerably less lurid than the layman has been led to believe. Certainly the typical analyst is anything but a lewd, sinful or gossip-loving man at heart. He is first of all a physician—and doctors are notoriously conservative, possibly because no frivolous man would want to burden himself with such a long and arduous course of study. For all the somewhat startling theory he accepts, in practice he is usually a solid and even stolid citizen, devoted to his family and his dog. (Freud always had a dog and sometimes two of them.) The good, middle-class orthodoxy of the analysts is in fact considered by some of them to be a serious weakness of their profession. The typical analyst, though he can understand and sympathize with the customary polite and restrained neuroses of the college-educated, may be lost altogether when it comes to dealing with the brutality, lust, drunkenness and crime that represent the common neurotic pattern among the lowest social classes. Very few analysts have ever managed to operate effectively in prisons or among slum area juvenile delinquents, even though these are areas where their services are desperately needed.

To understand how an analyst actually does go about treating his patients, all the popular misconceptions aside, it is necessary to grasp some of the principles of psychoanalytic theory. This is not easy. The book which is generally considered the shortest, simplest and easiest guide to the field, stripped down to the bare essentials, is Dr. Charles Brenner's *An Elementary Textbook of Psychoanalysis;* it is some fourteen times as long as this chapter and there are parts of it which even Dr. Brenner concedes must be read three or four or a half dozen times before they can be properly understood. The really basic concepts of psychoanalysis, however, can be summarized about as follows:

The most important Freudian principle of all is that of the unconscious. Freud was the first to point out the now generally accepted fact that the human mentality and personality are like an iceberg, so to speak, with only a small part visible and the great bulk submerged and concealed. In our everyday life we see countless examples. A mother claims to be the soul of generosity in her dealings with a daughter, motivated by the most self-sacrificing kind of love—yet we can see plainly that her real motive is to tie the daughter to her apron strings, dominate the girl, keep her from marrying and have her as a maidservant all her life. Or a man is a very pious churchgoer, a deacon, extremely strict with his wife and children—yet consistently tries to short-change his business associates. We sometimes think of such people as hypocrites, but more often than not they are simply the victims of a vast disparity between what they think they are and what their unconscious motives actually make them.

Perhaps an even better example of the unconscious is the phenomenon known as posthypnotic suggestion. The hypnotist tells the subject that after waking from his trance he will, without remembering this command, go and raise a window the first time the hypnotist coughs. Sure enough the subject does so. If you ask him why, he will invent some excuse, perhaps that the room felt stuffy—never suspecting that the real reason was completely unconscious. It is Freud's major premise that just as a forgotten hypnotic command can make us open a window without knowing why, so can all kinds of forgotten desires and conflicts affect our behavior without our ever knowing it.

The core of the unconscious is what Freud called the id. This is the raw, primitive, untrammeled, instinctive part of the human personality. According to Freud, the baby in its crib, unable as yet to think like a human being, more like a little animal, is a creature of boundless passions. It is swayed by two powerful, overwhelming drives. One is to love and to be loved, to be fondled and protected, to be kept warm and happy—all the feelings that are part of the complex pattern of behavior that centers around what adults know as the sex impulse. The other is to fight, to dominate and where necessary to destroy—in a word, to be aggressive. In the child, Freud says, these two drives know absolutely no limit. The id is blind, insatiable and urgent; it demands immediate and total satisfaction for its slightest whim; it will brook no delays and no obstacles. It wants to possess completely everything it loves; it wants to destroy anyone or anything that stands in its way. When it is frustrated it reacts with terrible and murderous rage. As the child grows up it learns to deal with and control these impulses—but the id remains active all our lives, a sort of beast within, crude and demanding, thinking in the primitive, illogical and often even wordless kind of way that makes our dreams so strange and foolish, or makes us rant and rave when we have a high fever.

The conscious, sensible part of the mind which develops as the child grows older was termed by Freud the ego. The ego is the real us as we think of ourselves. It does our logical thinking; it is alert to what goes on around us; it does the best it can to help us lead sane and satisfactory lives in relation to our environment. To the extent that the primitive drives of the id can be satisfied without harm or danger, the ego permits them satisfaction. But when the drives threaten to involve us in serious conflict—or get us jailed or shot—it holds them down. It has a number of ways of doing this. Of all the mechanisms by which the ego maintains our defenses against the ruinous demands of the id, the simplest and most important is repression. This means that the offending or dangerous wish and everything about it, the situation in which it welled up and the conflict it caused us, are actively pushed back into unconsciousness and kept there no matter how hard they struggle for expression; we never again become aware of them except insofar as they can creep in disguised form into our dreams or fantasies when our defenses are down.

In its constant struggle to keep the id in line, the ego has a strong but difficult ally in the third part of the mind as mapped by Freud—the superego. The superego is usually defined for the benefit of laymen as the conscience, that still small voice which tells us what is right and what is wrong. But this is a very superficial explanation. For one thing the superego is mostly or totally within the unconscious, like the id, and in a way its demands and its strictures are just as illogical and insatiable as the id's blind drives. Like the conscience we are aware of, it does set up standards of right and wrong—but it does this without our knowing it, and its standards are far more rigid, unrelenting, fierce and vengeful than anything in our conscious minds.

The superego is formed, as the child grows up, as a result of that famous conflict known as the Oedipus complex, which is perhaps the most widely publicized feature of the entire Freudian theory. Many people find the whole idea of the Oedipus conflict so distasteful and so distressing that they simply refuse to believe it, and therefore reject the whole structure of psychoanalysis. To analysts, however, the Oedipus complex is nothing shocking at all, but simply a natural and inevitable accompaniment of growing up, observed over and over again. They say that between the ages of about two and one-half to six every child is embroiled in a virtual frenzy of mingled love and hate for its parents, passions as strong as any it will ever feel in later life. The child has just begun to distinguish the outer world and to understand that there are people in it. So now the id's drive for sex and affection reaches out in-

71

satiably toward the first object at hand. Though the boy baby has only the haziest notions and feelings of what sex is all about, he wants to possess his mother utterly and totally insofar as he comprehends this; his love for her knows no bounds. Nor does his rage against his father, the hated rival with whom he must share her. But his very rage makes him afraid that his father will somehow retaliate, and his every move is fraught with fear. To complicate matters, his insatiable demands for love from his mother are of course denied and now the aggressive drive of his id also springs into action toward her; while loving her beyond reason he also hates her and determines to take her place with the father—so that now he is over-whelmed with mingled love, hate and fear for both parents at once. Girls go through almost the same torments, except that their affection centers chiefly on their fathers, their feelings of rivalry on their mothers.

This period of horrible storm and stress must somehow be resolved. One of the mechanisms by which this happens is identification—another important psychoanalytic term—with the parents. This is not an easy process to describe; in brief it means that the child more or less absorbs his parents into his own personality—especially the more for-bidding and disciplinary aspects of his parents. He solves his mingled love and hate for them by becoming like them, by taking into himself their strength and their authority, by convincing himself that his love and hate are "bad." Their moral judgments, or what he conceives of as their moral judgments, now become his superego. This helps him hold back the id drives which caused him such intense discomfort during the Oedipal period. But forever after the superego will to a certain extent dominate him. As his parents once did, it will punish him or threaten to punish him for transgressions. And since its standards were rigidly set in childhood, its notions of crime and guilt are likely to be completely illogical and unduly harsh.

This, then, is in much simplified terms the structure of the human mind as conceived by Freud—the conscious ego trying to keep our behavior on some sort of sensible and even keel, and doing the best it can to satisfy some of the drives of the insatiable id without incurring the wrath and vengeance of the implacable superego. The chances for something to go wrong with this delicate balance of power are almost infinite. For example if a person's ego cannot set up adequate defenses and the id's drives are insufficiently checked, he is unfit to be a member of society, or at least of polite society; he will be a rake and a hot-headed brawler. If on the other hand the defenses are too strong, he may get into subtler but equally distasteful problems. Too much repression of the sex drives renders a person unable to enjoy a normal sex life or express and receive a normal amount of affection as an adult. Too much repression of the aggressive drive makes him unable to stand up for himself, to hold his own in the give and take of competition. Too strict a superego will flood his entire life with vague and unwarranted feelings of guilt and unworthiness. This is the cause of what is often called, though Freud did not introduce the term, the "inferiority complex."

To the extent that a person's behavior is controlled by

the conscious aspect of his mind—the ego—it is sensible, satisfying and normal. To the extent that behavior is governed by childish passions and prejudices of his unconscious—the dark and primitive urges of the id and the rigid and unrelenting demands of the superego—it tends to be foolish, unrewarding, painful and neurotic. What the analyst tries to do when treating a neurotic patient, therefore, is to bring as much as possible of the unconscious out into view, to dredge up all the old repressed urges and conflicts and subject them to the scrutiny of the patient's conscious mind. Once they have become a matter of conscious knowledge and control, they lose their ability to terrorize the patient and to drive him into erratic behavior.

The chief tool of the analyst is the technique, also evolved by Freud, known as free association. The analyst urges the patient, while lying as relaxed as possible on a couch, to let his mind wander where it will—and to speak up with every thought that occurs to him, no matter how foolish or irrelevant it may seem, or indeed how undignified, insulting to the analyst or even obscene. Under these circumstances, much as when drifting off to sleep or dreaming during sleep, conscious control of the workings of the mind is reduced to a minimum, and the unconscious forces have their greatest opportunity to make themselves known, at least by indirection. To the extent that the patient can remember his dreams, the interpretation of which is another complex branch of psychoanalysis, these are also reported. Gradually the analyst gets a picture in depth of the patient's mental processes and problems, not only the conscious ones which are apparent on the surface but also the unconscious ones which have been buried since earliest childhood.

The couch is used in analysis partly to relax the patient and partly to place him in a position where he can be observed by the analyst, who sits to one side and the rear, without being able to watch the analyst in turn. This is part of the mantle of anonymity which has already been mentioned as desirable on the part of the analyst. If the analyst were in view the patient could not help responding to his facial expressions, whether these indicated approval, disapproval or merely a stony inscrutability. But what the analyst has to get at is the patient's own intrinsic trends of thought, unaffected by such extraneous matters. Similarly the analyst conceals his own personality, his own likes and dislikes, so that any reactions the patient has toward him will reflect the patient's own basic personality, unaffected by anything the analyst himself is or does.

How the patient behaves toward the analyst involves the phenomenon called transference, another of the well-known but frequently misunderstood principles of psychoanalysis. It is a common misconception that toward the end of an analysis the patient transfers his emotions to the analyst—usually, in the case of women patients, by falling in love with him—and that this burst of emotion suddenly frees the patient from all crippling restraint. Actually transference is something quite different. It simply means that all of us in our adult lives tend to transfer to everyone we meet the emotional attitudes that we once felt toward such much loved and hated persons as our parents and our sisters and brothers. These old, repressed and unconscious loves and hates often make us have the deepest sort of affection for people whom our intellects tell us are quite unworthy (like the love affair of the hero in *Of Human Bondage*) or despise people for no sensible reason at all. In analysis, patients seeing their doctor day after day and pouring out their thoughts to him naturally are moved to these spontaneous emotional reactions; they are frequently overwhelmed by a desire to please him and be praised by him or by a wild resentment and hatred of him, or a mixture of both. Since the doctor has done his best to be neither likable nor dislikable, these feelings obviously spring from the deepest layers of the patient's own personality and afford a good clue to his unconscious. Moreover the analyst does not discourage them but lets them develop fully so that they can be studied. Once the analyst has helped the patient understand their sources, the battle is more than half won.

The progress of an analysis, however, is usually slow and painful. It is very hard for anyone to lie on a couch and let his mind wander unguided through free associations while at the same time putting these thoughts into words—and it is especially hard for the seriously neurotic person because so many areas of thought are blocked by what are called resistances, his unconscious inability to approach any of his repressed memories. If a patient could get right down to free associating during the very first session, and do so regularly for the entire hour on every subsequent day, psychoanalysis would be neither lengthy nor terribly expensive and everybody would be much happier. Unfortunately very little of the analytic hour, some-times no more than a few minutes in the course of an entire week, is actually spent in this manner. The rest is waste motion.

Yet there is little the analyst can do to hasten the process. If he asks leading questions, he puts at least a temporary end to any possibility of free associations. If he talks psy-choanalytical theory, he puts the analysis on too intellectual a plane and runs the risk that the patient will learn the language of analysis without ever learning its personal meaning. He cannot even speed matters along by telling the patient some of the obvious facts he has already learned about the patient's personality. As uncountable thou-sands of parents, teachers and clergymen have learned— or should have learned—it does no good to reason with a stubborn child, a drunk, a gambler or a young woman consumed by an ill-advised love. Until the neurotic patient has himself caught an insight into his problems, it may only make things worse to tell him what is wrong. So the analyst can only wait; it has been said that he must resign himself to letting the patient maintain day after day that two and two are five until patient and analyst eventually discover together why the patient has believed this was so.

Here lies another common misconception about anal-ysis. Especially in the movies, psychoanalysts are forever urging their patients to take up a hobby, talk back to the boss or divorce an unsympathetic wife. In truth analysts lean over backward to avoid the slightest semblance of such a thing. At the start of an analysis they usually ask the patient to refrain from shifting jobs, getting married or divorced or making any other serious change while treatment is in progress. This is partly because any major decision might temporarily alter the patient's whole mood and delay the successful treatment of his inward problems, but mostly because the stresses and strains of analysis itself may incline the patient toward impetuous actions which he would later regret. As for advice in the course of treatment, analysts believe that they could not offer it without revealing some of their own attitudes and preferences and thus losing their anonymity. Moreover the neurotic patient can only react to such advice with blind childish dependence or blind childish rebellion, which would only add to his real problems. The psychological counselor or the nonanalytic psychiatrist may sometimes decide that certain people can be helped with sound advice if their neurotic difficulties are not too serious—but the analyst never does.

There is another popular notion that the ultimate end of the psychoanalysis comes in a sort of sudden blinding flash. The patient stumbles on the memory of some painful childhood experience, like accidentally being locked in the bathroom at the age of two, he tells the doctor all about this old memory—and lo and behold he is a new man. There is even a name for this with which many laymen are familiar: catharsis. It so happens that the word was often used by Freud, who found early in the game that patients could sometimes be cured of blindness or paralysis that stemmed from emotional upset rather than physical causes by being induced under hypnosis to recall and talk about an event that had profoundly disturbed them. Freud soon discovered, however, that the basic neurotic problem remained and only the symptom was banished by catharsis, more likely than not to crop up in a new form some time later. The same principle holds true of all neuroses. A patient may get some temporary relief by admitting out loud for the first time his secret hatred of a younger brother, or by recalling his terror as a child at witnessing some scene of brutality or lust. But the "catharsis" does not solve his problems.

What does finally help him in the successful analysis, or at least reduce the number of tempestuous unconscious conflicts and increase the areas in which he has conscious understanding of himself, is something much more gradual and much less spectacular. The analyst, attuned to unconscious problems, begins to get a fairly clear picture of what is really bothering the patient. Some of his clues come from the free associations and the dreams; some come from his interpretation of the patient's transference, and others come from the very things which the patient avoids because of his resistances. Gradually the analyst leads the patient to understand that perhaps the reason he suffered a stomach upset the previous afternoon was that he had met the company president in the elevator after lunch. But why should the boss frighten him so? And there the trail begins to lead slowly back to all sorts of forgotten memories and emotional storms, perhaps to his childish fear of his father's retaliation during his Oedipal period, perhaps to the formation of an overstrict superego which will never forgive him for having failed to rise to become boss himself, perhaps both of these and many more.

The layers within layers seem endless; the patient despairs of ever really comprehending the conflicts within him. But gradually it all falls into place; the analyst helps the patient catch a glimpse of how ancient, forgotten wishes and fears persist in his unconscious mind and haunt his life; eventually he gains control of the unconscious drives and conflicts and they bedevil him no more. He has won what an analyst named Dr. Lawrence S. Kubie has called the finest gift that psychoanalysis can bestow: "freedom from the tyranny of the unconscious."

This is the goal of analysis. It is not always attained and some critics say it never can be through analytic methods, as we shall see in the next chapter. But it is the greatest of all the great hopes which our psychological age holds out to a struggling humanity.

CHAPTER FIVE

Does Psychoanalysis Work?

IN TRYING to make any sensible evaluation of psychoanalysis, the most common criticisms can be thrown out right at the start. The analyst, more than any other professional man except possibly the politician, has to accept gratuitous insult as a routine occupational hazard. His successes go unnoticed, while his failures fairly shout for attention. The patients for whom he has done the most usually go about their business quietly, and nobody except possibly a few close friends ever knows they have been analyzed. The patients for whom he has done the least are often quite vocal, and give analysis a bad name by boring their acquaintances half to death with dubious analytical lore. Among those who visit the analyst's office are a great many people who he knows are headed for the gravest sort of mental problems but who as yet seem only the tiniest bit odd to their families. If he treats such a patient successfully, the family is likely to think that there was nothing wrong in the first place—the treatment was just an expensive racket. If he fails and the patient has to go to a mental hospital, he gets the full blame—the patient was all right until the analyst got hold of him. And so it goes. Were analysts not so thoroughly analyzed themselves, they would doubtless all have persecution complexes.

Psychoanalysis has also been attacked on a number of quite legitimate grounds, however, by many competent and thoughtful critics. Their most telling points can be summarized about as follows:

Freud's so-called "discoveries" are merely theories and nothing more, completely unprovable by any laboratory methods. Nobody has ever yet seen a human id, ego or superego under a microscope and nobody ever will. All we have to go on is the unsupported word of Freud himself. True, his followers claim that his findings are "proved" by their observations of patients, but Freud's followers are too prejudiced to trust. Naturally any man who undergoes analytic training—all those long years of indoctrination and that intimate process known as analysis at the hands of a Freudian—is bound to be pretty well brainwashed in Freud's favor. If an analyst decided at the end of his training that he had wasted all his years from twenty to thirty-five on nonsense, what would he do for a living?

As to Freud's reliability as an observer, one need only

look at the record—for example, at the definitive biography of Freud (*The Life and Work of Sigmund Freud*, Basic Books, New York) which has been written by his first English-speaking disciple, Dr. Ernest A. Jones, who remained a close friend until Freud's death in 1939. The biography is completely sympathetic; indeed it is Dr. Jones's contention that Freud's discoveries were "the nearest to a miracle that human means can encompass." Yet it contains the strongest sort of evidence that Freud was at times very gullible. There is, for example, the matter of his long friendship with a strange and mystical Berlin doctor named Wilhelm Fliess. Dr. Fliess had a theory that all human events, including birth and death, are governed by the numbers *23* and *28*. When these numbers failed him, as of course they frequently did, he went on all undaunted to add them, subtract them, multiply and juggle them until he finally proved his point. It was the most palpable kind of hocus-pocus, a sort of "science" of numerology for which only the most naïve Hollywood actresses are supposed to fall. Yet Freud took it seriously, and for years believed Dr. Fliess's prediction that he would die at the age of fifty-one. When this year came and went and he remained miraculously alive, he somehow settled on a new superstition, this time without any help from Dr. Fliess, that he would die in February 1918, a date premature by twenty-one years.

Psychoanalysts claim to be alert to the patient's hidden thoughts and meanings; they pride themselves on being adept at the process which the eminent analyst Theodor Reik has described in a book title as *Listening with the*

Third Ear. Freud's third ear, still according to the evidence in Dr. Jones's biography as interpreted by his critics, was quite deaf at times. Biographer Jones concedes that in the course of one analysis by Freud, of a patient whom Jones happened to know very well, he found "instance after instance" where Freud swallowed statements which Jones knew to be untrue and refused to believe things that definitely were true. Jones also cites an incident where a new patient complained to Freud that she had been shamefully mistreated by an analyst named Dr. Blank in Ipswich, England. Freud became extremely angry and told the story with great annoyance to a British woman student with whom he met during the next hour. The student caught on at once that the patient had invented the entire tale, as neurotics so often will. She pointed out tactfully that there was no Dr. Blank in England and had never been an analyst by any name in Ipswich, but these facts made absolutely no impression on Freud. He continued to be painfully aggrieved at the mythical Dr. Blank until he finally got a belated letter from a colleague who had sent the woman patient to him—explaining that she was a confirmed paranoiac with a specialty of claiming mistreatment by her doctors.

As a youngish doctor Freud was much impressed by how often his patients appeared to have been seduced in childhood—the women by their fathers or uncles, the men by a nursemaid. He therefore formulated the theory that all neurosis was caused by the traumatic experience (i.e., a shock causing lasting injury to the mental processes) of sexual mistreatment as a child. This was his firm conviction for about four years, at a time when he was in his late thirties, until he eventually discovered that his patients had only made up these stories, too. He then abandoned his theory and started all over on the paths which led to his final concepts. But every psychologist is familiar with the phenomenon known as mental "set." For instance, if someone spells out to you the names *Mac-Phail, MacPherson, MacDougall* and then slips in the common word *machinery,* you will almost surely mispronounce it, because your mind is "set" for the *Mac* sound. Similarly Freud's early theories, based on his failure to distinguish facts from fantasy, doubtless persisted as an influence in his later findings about the sexual drive of infants and the Oedipus complex. He had his mind set on a sexual explanation from the start and saw in his patients what he was prepared to see. Moreover it was easy to get them to confirm his expectations, for neurotics are a suggestible lot and will develop new symptoms and even new histories at the drop of a hint.

The opponents of analysis also say that Freudianism can make only the most doubtful of claims for any curative value. Certainly there is strong evidence, again right in the Jones biography, that the first patient of all retained a number of neurotic traits to the end of his days despite all his intensive self-analysis. Freud was addicted to cigar smoking—twenty a day—and suffered the most intense kind of psychosomatic symptoms when he tried to stop. He was something of a hypochondriac in general; his letters to friends were full of complaints about such matters, again surely psychosomatic, as constipation, poor digestion and heart palpitation. He was extremely worried about traveling and the worst kind of nervous Nellie about getting to the station long before train time. In his professional life he was inclined to be somewhat quarrelsome and quite indiscreet about confidential information he received from his associates.

Analysts since Freud have also had their difficulties. For proof that psychoanalysis is no 100 per cent guarantee of equanimity even for its experts, one need only read Dr. Reik's *Fragment of a Great Confession,* in which he tells how he became overwhelmed by personal problems after twenty-five years as a practicing analyst, and had himself analyzed all over again. And anyone who knows a lot of analysts will testify that the ranks contain a full quota, just like any other human group, of those who lose their tempers, bark at their children, cheat at golf or try to make love to every woman they meet. There is no evidence that schools and departments of psychoanalysis are any better run than the average, or any freer from jealousy and intramural politicking. Psychoanalysts' children misbehave like any others. If the analysts can't cure themselves, how can they hope to cure anybody?

These are the theoretical arguments against psychoanalysis. There is also one very practical objection. A complete analysis requires that the patient manage to get away from his duties for an hour a day plus traveling time to and from the doctor's office, three to five times a week for two to five years. It costs anywhere from $7,000 to $25,000 and up. How many people even have the time, not to mention the money? Even if the world should become sufficiently leisurely and wealthy, how could we train enough analysts to go around? As things stand now, only a small minority of people even live anywhere near an analyst's office—and perhaps one in a hundred can afford to go. If the world has to wait for psychoanalysis to save it, most of us are doomed.

The case against psychoanalysis is a strong one; it cannot easily be brushed aside. How then do the analysts answer it?

They answer it, most of them at least, with a surprising modesty. Analysts are not, though they have been so advertised by some of the noisier ones, a bunch of know-it-alls. They are, by and large, a most moderate and even diffident group, and it is only a relatively few extremists among them who seem so cocksure and so contemptuous of criticism. Every time one of these extremists gets up in public and states categorically that comic books are the cause of juvenile delinquency, or testifies in court that he has been watching the defendant stare at the ceiling and can positively guarantee that the fellow is a psychopath, the more conservative analysts wince.

Most analysts would concede that the Freudian theories are unprovable by usual scientific standards, but would maintain that the theories have to be accepted because there is no other way to explain what is now a considerable body of human observation. Whatever Freud's intellectual weaknesses in other directions, he was a genius at achieving pioneer insights into the depths of human character, and his findings have been verified time and time again in the treatment of many thousands of patients. Perhaps he was somewhat gullible at times, as his critics claim, but he caught his errors in the long run and was far freer than most people to admit them and abandon them—as when he completely dropped Wilhelm Fliess. Indeed even his naïveté was an asset in that it enabled him to explore and finally find the right answer to problems which a less imaginative man might have ignored.

On the personal side, it is certainly true that Freud retained some obvious neuroticisms all his life, but surely no fair critic could deny that his self-analysis was none-theless of infinite value to him. He rid himself completely of the deep anxieties and depressions which marked his youth. In his adult, post-analytic life he did an enormous amount of work, which is one good practical measure of mental health, and made a considerable number of long-term friends, which is another. His family life, though run along lines which would perhaps seem old-fashioned and patriarchal now, was unusually free and spontaneous for Victorian days. Biographer Jones, who witnessed it, claims that it was in fact a model of warmth and affection un-marred by anything ever resembling a family scene. Granted that Freud had his idiosyncrasies, these were of a minor sort which—at least before his time—would have been considered any man's due.

The majority of analysts cheerfully grant that they them-selves probably possess certain eccentricities and that their colleagues certainly do. But this, they say, is only to be expected. In this imperfect state of mankind, it naturally happens that a good many college students are highly disturbed. Many such students have been attracted to the study of psychoanalysis because they have hoped to find there the answer to their own problems. Some few have gone on to practice psychoanalysis even though they have not managed to do much about their own peculiarities. Others have found part of the answer but not all, for psychoanalysis can hardly hope at this stage of its development for perfect results. In the broad sense none of this is bad in itself, because in all probability a person who has suffered neurotic problems of his own makes a better and more sensitive analyst than a person whose entire life has been one gay round of triumph and backslapping. Unfortunately some people have been permitted to practice analysis who never should have been—but this is being remedied with the new generation of analysts, who are weeded out by their teachers if they show signs of lacking the proper temperament and stability.

In attempting to assess how much they have managed to help their patients, the more conservative analysts always bear in mind that they are operating in a field where a certain number of cures have been effected for centuries by witch doctors, medicine men, magic waters and sugar pills. Every analyst can certainly cite from his own experience a number of cases where patients came to analysis disturbed, unhappy and barely able to carry on, and went away full of vigor and optimism. The question is how many of these patients would have shown the same marvelous improvement with different treatment, or without any treatment at all. There are no reliable figures and probably no way of ever getting any. As one analyst explained recently, "It's all right for our critics to talk about statistics and control groups and I wish too that we had them. But we're the fellows who have to keep the patient from jumping out a window. We don't have time to think in those terms."

Certainly the statistics, if kept, would show anything but 100 per cent success. Freud himself conceded that analysis was not very effective with really badly disturbed people like the schizophrenics who constitute the largest group of mental hospital inmates. Even among the merely neurotic, analysis has spotty results. It seems to have its best chance of success if the patient is quite young and if his difficulties are causing him sufficient discomfort to give him a strong motive for improvement. (In many cases, it is the neurotic's family that suffers while he himself goes rather gaily on his warped way; this type of patient seldom really wants to change matters.) Some analysts have considerably more success than others. All of this has led one prominent analyst, an extremist of the opposite type from those who usually get public notice, to make this private evaluation of psychoanalysis: "*If* what's troubling you isn't too serious, and *if* you're lucky enough to go to one of the few analysts who seem to be good at what they're doing, and *if* you're a good patient and work hard, then *maybe* analysis can help you."

Saints and teaching geniuses have always had the knack of comforting and enriching the lives of others with whom they came into intimate contact, long before Freud was ever born. The hope of psychoanalysis, which keeps it going and growing, is that it is a tool which can help human unfortunates and add to human happiness even in the hands of men who are less than saints and geniuses. All analysts, even the most conservative, feel that they have certainly managed to accomplish a great deal under the pioneering circumstances. They also believe that the art of analysis is constantly being improved, and that the new generation of analysts will probably accomplish far more than the old. For one thing the newcomers have grown up in an atmosphere which takes analysis for granted; for another the teaching methods have greatly improved. Students can now profit from a psychoanalytical literature which was just starting to accumulate a generation ago and from countless analytic sessions, fruitful or futile, which have been recorded on tape or movie film for study at leisure. One teacher of analysis said recently, "These students we have now are just as keen and sensitive to the patient's problems at twenty-five as we were at forty."

There are some psychoanalysts who themselves have discarded much of the Freudian theory, even while continuing to agree in general with the efficacy of his approach to the treatment of mental problems. The two most famous rebels from within the ranks were Alfred Adler and Carl Jung, who were among Freud's earliest followers and broke away from him at about the same time—roughly the year 1911 and the months immediately following—to found rival schools of their own. Their defections caused considerable turmoil within the psychoanalytic movement, which was of course much smaller then than now, and for a time the whole future course of the movement seemed shrouded in doubt.

Adler found himself unwilling to believe Freud's theories of the sexual origins of neurosis, and came to feel that the entire Freudian doctrine was far too vague and complex. As he saw it, all adult human psychology, normal or abnormal, revolves around the fact that a baby is born into the world completely helpless, utterly dependent on those around it and therefore filled with the most profound feelings of inferiority. All later life is an attempt to achieve a sense of superiority to make up for these early inadequacies. Where development is normal, the growing child acquires such virtues as courage, independence and wholesome ambition. Where development is thwarted by unsympathetic parents or by a defect such as lameness or stuttering, the growing child can get into all sorts of neurotic difficulties. He may become overwhelmed by feelings of inadequacy— a victim of that famous Adlerian concept, the "inferiority complex." Or he may become overly ambitious and aggressive in a destructive sense. Adler's theories of the cause of neurosis were much simpler than Freud's and so were his methods of helping patients. He felt that the most important thing was to lead the patient to understand the struggle between his urge for superiority and his feelings of inferiority and then help the patient to resolve the struggle by sympathetic guidance and encouragement.

Jung, on the other hand, is even more complex than Freud. He, too, refuses to believe in the sexual origin of neurosis, but he seeks the causes in far more subtle and even mystic matters. Jung believes every man's life is deeply influenced by a "collective unconscious" which is his heritage from thousands of years of mankind's struggles. The collective unconscious is a reservoir of all the attitudes our ancient ancestors had toward life and death, toward religion, toward virtue and sin. It is full of such symbols as the Good Mother who protects us, the Terrible Mother who casts us out into the dangers of life, and the magic circle which throughout mankind's history has represented a full and balanced existence. Neurotic problems are a sign of failure to integrate all these age-old strivings, and the solution lies in attaining an understanding in depth of how we have failed to express ourselves and to fulfill our destinies.

Jung, who is now eighty-one but still active, has had a considerable appeal over the years to people who liked the general idea of psychoanalysis but found Freud too concerned with sex and too oblivious of man's religious impulses. Adler, who died in 1937, has had a considerable vogue among those who found Freud too complicated. (Freudians sometimes call Adler a "kindergarten psychologist.") There are a number of Jungians and Adlerians still practicing, writing and training new followers. Their influence, however, has waned rather than increased over the years, and they have never got beyond the status of splinter groups as far as numerical strength is concerned.

In recent years some other new schools of psychoanalysis have been founded, representing breaks of greater or lesser degree from Freudian theory. Among the best known of them are the Karen Horney group and the Harry Stack Sullivan group, both of which place less emphasis than did Freud on the patient's instinctual drives and more on his present problems. Dr. Horney, for example, in writing a series of books about her developing theories, never once mentioned any such thing as ego, id, superego or Oedipus complex, and seldom used the word *sex*. Her books, which are relatively easy for a layman to read, have had a wide sale, and her followers have set up a clinic named in her honor in New York City. Nonetheless all the non-Freudian schools put together still constitute a rather small minority, and orthodox Freudianism remains the dominant school of thought in the analytic movement. Its friends say it has thrived because it represents the most inspiring and illuminating approach yet to the murky secrets of the human personality.

CHAPTER SIX

The Other Approaches to Mental Health

THERE are about 9,000 practicing U. S. psychiatrists who are not psychoanalysts. Some of them believe strongly in the principles of analysis and some are completely skeptical. Others have never even had time to make up their minds—for the nonanalytic psychiatrists are the front-line troops in the battle against mental disease, kept hopping all day and often all night by the explosions around them. Most psychoanalysts are in private practice and carefully select their patients, limiting their treatment to cases where it can be expected to be most helpful. In contrast, most nonanalytic psychiatrists do the bulk of their work in mental hospitals and clinics where they see all kinds of patients and especially the most difficult ones.

95

In the course of a single day the typical psychiatrist may be called upon to treat a mentally retarded infant who suffered an oxygen lack before birth, a young woman with early symptoms of schizophrenia and an old man succumbing to senile dementia. Faced with such a wide range of problems, the psychiatrist has become mental health's great eclectic—he uses any techniques that seem useful, and sometimes uses them even though he is not quite sure whether to believe them.

The psychiatrists have adopted many of the concepts and methods of the analysts, as well as many of the findings of the psychologists. They also use a wide variety of physiological methods and medicines. A good example of the way they work is the treatment they gave to battle-fatigued soldiers during World War II. The typical psychiatrist first put the soldier under sedation for a couple of days, to make the most of the well-known value of sleep in repairing the human organism. He then tried narco-analysis in which a drug like sodium amytal (a "truth serum") is administered to produce a flow of talk and free associations. He followed this with a fairly simple form of psychotherapy—merely explaining to the soldier that fear is a normal human emotion involving definite, useful but sometimes highly unpleasant changes in the body. If the soldier was badly underweight as a result of inability to eat or to keep food down, the psychiatrist prescribed intravenous feedings, small doses of insulin to stimulate appetite or other pharmacological methods of building up the body tissue. If all this failed to bring about any improvement, he then resorted to deeper psychotherapy, something like a short form of psychoanalysis.

Speaking in the most general terms, the psychiatrist considers all patients "battle fatigued." He believes that all of us are limited in the amount of strain we can stand. Our limits are set by the constitutions we have inherited and by the way we have solved or failed to solve the emotional problems of growing up. As a practical matter, the psychiatrist tries to keep his treatment as short as possible. His concept of a cure is a pragmatic one: he thinks in terms of getting the patient in shape to carry on his daily affairs successfully. He does not try to bring about a total understanding and integration in the psychoanalytic sense—which he tends to consider an impossible goal anyway.

Usually the psychiatrist is much more interested than the analyst in such things as the patient's job, working conditions, marriage and children. Where the analyst's ideal is to make the patient capable of functioning well in practically any environment, the psychiatrist often tries to shore up the patient by taking some of the strains out of the existing environment. He does this, in most cases, with the help of that new and valuable aide called the psychiatric social worker. Especially in dealing with the lowest-income groups, the psychiatrist would tend to say that often the patient cannot be expected to improve at all unless the physical and financial circumstances of his life can somehow be bettered. Likewise many psychiatrists believe that the greatest hope for preventing and alleviating the mental ills of old age lies with the sociologist, for the thing the aged needs most is a continuing sense of usefulness and participation in the community.

The problem of mental health is also being attacked on a broad front today by the clinical psychologists, who are indeed the fastest-growing group in the field. In recent years about 40 per cent of all graduate students in psychology have been specializing in the clinical branch, and it is expected that clinical psychologists will soon outnumber the psychiatrists and psychoanalysts. The clinical psychologists have developed a number of new methods of their own; they have experimented widely, for example, with techniques called "play therapy," in which children are urged to express and tackle their emotional problems in their drawings and relations with their toys, and "psychodrama," in which disturbed persons are urged to act out the conflicts they cannot talk about. One prominent clinical psychologist, Dr. C. R. Rogers, reports considerable success with what he has called "client-centered therapy," the chief feature of which is the therapist's attempt to assume an attitude of complete sympathy and encouragement for his client, thus providing an emotional atmosphere in which the disturbed person can flourish and solve his own problems.

Clinical psychologists have also done a good deal of work in diagnosing mental problems and devising tests to reveal them. The Rorschach ink-blot test of personality is the most famous of the devices of this type invented by the psychologists, and there are many others. Much of the future research into the causes, nature and relief of mental problems will probably also be done by the psychologists. By the nature of their training, psychologists are oriented from the start toward laboratory research and the keeping and interpretation of statistics. Psychiatrists and analysts, on the other hand, are mostly concerned from the very beginning with the use of their knowledge as an art of healing.

To a certain extent, all the fine work being done in the field of psychotherapy has been obscured recently by the great publicity given the purely medical approach to mental illness. The theory that mental ills are essentially a reflection of some abnormal physical condition has appealed to many observers for years, and has received a considerable boost from the sudden fame of the tranquilizing drugs like reserpine and chlorpromazine. Like all new developments in the field of mental health, the tranquilizing drugs have probably enjoyed a fad somewhat beyond their real significance. There is no evidence that they get at the causes of the psychoses, and therefore no reason to hope that they have brought us any closer to a complete understanding of mental illness. But they do bring about an often spectacular improvement in the behavior and lucidity of the mentally ill, to the point where patients are much easier to handle in institutions and often can even get along in society. They are, at any rate, certainly the most dramatic of the recent additions to a considerable body of evidence that some, most or even all psychoses have an essentially physical or chemical basis and may some day be cured by the proper drugs.

If mankind's emotional ills had no physical cause whatever, and were strictly a product of the particular stresses and strains of a particular society, one would expect them to vary greatly from time to time through history and from place to place. But records of the early Massachusetts courts show that there were just as many commitments to mental hospitals, in proportion to population, in the quiet and more rural Massachusetts of the nineteenth century as in the speeded-up industrial Massachusetts of today. A study of the old-fashioned island of Bornholm off the coast of Denmark, an eighteenth-century type of society, completely isolated from the hurly-burly of our modern civilization, has shown the same types of psychosis and neurosis found in our most frantic cities. In fact anthropologists say they have found familiar patterns of mental aberrations in every society and culture they have ever studied.

Some of the statistics on heredity, although never very widely kept, also seem to argue for a physical basis. Some famous studies by Dr. Franz Kallmann indicate that if a parent has schizophrenia his children are sixteen times as likely as the average person to have it. Among identical twins Kallmann found that when one is schizophrenic the other is too in 86 per cent of cases, and when one twin has manic-depressive psychosis the other does too in 96 per cent of cases. The only question is to what extent these figures reflect the effects of sheer heredity and to what extent the effects of a bad family environment. What is needed to resolve the argument is a group of cases of identical twins reared in different households, but these have been too rare to date to provide any positive proof.

Aside from theoretical speculation, it is a matter of hard fact that a considerable number of mental disturbances of various types have already been definitely traced to physical causes. Among them are paresis (caused by the syphilis spirochete), dementia of the aged (caused by constricted blood vessels and deteriorating brain cells) and the psychosis accompanying pellagra (a disease caused by a vitamin deficiency). Drugs have been developed to combat epilepsy and a hormone has been found to prevent cretinism.

A number of experimenters are now doing research along lines suggested by the work of Dr. Hans Selye of the University of Montreal, an endocrinologist or gland expert who has become famous in recent years for his work on what he calls "nonspecific stress." What Dr. Selye says, in brief, is this: that everything we do and everything that happens to us, from the normal effort of work and play to an attack by bacteria, creates a condition of stress inside the body. Our physical apparatus goes to work either to facilitate the effort, adjust to the change or repair the damage. The "stress apparatus," as Dr. Selye sees it, is chiefly regulated by the pituitary and adrenal glands, but also involves the nervous system, heart, lungs, stomach, liver, kidneys and lymph glands. When the system is working properly we get along fine and are impervious even to bacteria that might make us sick under less efficient conditions. When we are under a severe or prolonged strain of some sort, the over- or under-functioning of the stress apparatus itself may lead to physical ailments or perhaps mental disturbances as well.

A happy thought or a worried thought affects the stress apparatus; likewise the complicated body chemistry of the stress apparatus must surely have an effect upon the brain. It is, for example, Dr. Selye's present hunch—though no more than a hunch—that the secret of schizophrenia may be some apparently harmless chemical which is quite naturally and normally produced in the brain by the working of the nerve cells and the burning of food. He presumes that it would be a chemical which has no effect on people whose stress apparatus is working properly, but causes insanity when the apparatus is out of kilter and changes the body's chemistry in some as yet unknown way.

All this evidence and speculation about drugs suggest some interesting possibilities. Perhaps most mental problems have a direct physical cause for which we shall some day have a medicine. Perhaps the psychoses have a direct physical basis but the minor neurotic problems do not—which could mean that psychiatrists might some day be in the ironic position of today's general practitioners, fine at curing pneumonia but unable to make much headway against the common cold. Or the physical and psychological aspects may be so intermingled that, like the chicken and the egg, it will always be impossible to say which came first.

Freud himself felt—though some of his followers seem to have forgotten it—that there had to be some kind of close relationship between psychiatry and physical medicine; he said that behind the psychoanalyst stands the man with the syringe. Certainly the new burst of interest in mental ills among the physical scientists—biochemists,

physiologists, pharmacologists, neurologists and others—
holds great promise. In the opinion of some experts it
heralds a major breakthrough. A great deal of optimism
for the future has been engendered, for example, by the
work at Yale of Dr. José Delgado, who has been learning
all sorts of new facts about the functioning of various
centers of the brain.

To anyone who is a close reader of the science columns
in the newspapers and news magazines these days, it must
often seem as if the breakthrough has already been made.
At various times in recent months, for example, scientists
have reported the discovery of a blood test which reveals
schizophrenia, or the isolation of a chemical substance in
the blood of schizophrenics which will cause symptoms
of the disease when injected into normal persons. Unfortunately this is a branch of biochemistry involving the
most subtle and difficult problems, and the result that one
experimenter gets today may never occur again when the
same experiment is tried by other scientists. Moreover mankind's desire for a sure cure to mental ills is so strong
that each new discovery, however tentative, tends to be
magnified out of all proportion. Many startling findings
have been reported in the past and taken up as fads only
to prove a complete disappointment over the long term,
and the same thing will doubtless often happen again.

Even if the breakthrough is not yet close at hand, the
fact remains that the struggle for mental health has already
come a long way. Even psychiatrists not yet past middle
age can remember when the only real difference between

what they considered an average mental hospital and a bad one was that in the average hospital the patients were beaten less frequently. In those days, two or three decades ago, the typical hospital was staffed by a politically appointed superintendent, usually without any special training; by a group of guards chosen for their physical strength; by a few psychiatrists valiantly trying to introduce the most elementary reforms; and perhaps by one pioneer psychologist and by one social worker just beginning to learn the ropes.

Today, although most mental hospitals are still understaffed, the differences are amazing. The whole level of competence has risen rapidly. The old brutality is vanishing. In more and more hospitals the psychiatrists and psychologists now have time, though not nearly so much as they wish they had, for a good bit of personal care, testing and therapy. The well-trained psychiatric nurse, male and female alike, is replacing the old strong-arm guard—and is becoming one of the unsung heroes of the line. Even the least wealthy and most overcrowded hospitals are in at least one sense ahead of the general public. Every hospital has a number of patients, sometimes a great many of them, who have progressed to the point where they could easily be sent home—except that their families do not want them home.

The current trend, which will doubtless continue even if there are no major discoveries in the next few years, is for psychiatry to move out of the mental hospital and into the community. The new place of the psychiatrist, the psychoanalyst, the clinical psychologist—and of their new partners, the psychiatric nurses and psychiatric social work-ers—is in everyday private work or in community clinics. At the same time more and more clergymen and teachers are becoming wise in the ways of psychology. Public health officials and organizations like the National Association for Mental Health are helping spread the gospel, especially among families of mental patients.

Psychiatrists are experimenting with all kinds of short-cut methods of helping the emotionally disturbed. Even some of the analysts, although traditionally committed to the 1,000-hour type of treatment, are trying out a much briefer, accelerated type of therapy. Some are experimenting with group therapy, in which they treat perhaps a half-dozen patients who discuss their problems back and forth. Many of them feel that the greatest opportunity of all may lie in the area of preventive psychology and psychiatry, perhaps a new science of child rearing and youth education which will keep conflicts from developing. Studies of orphans and the temporary orphans who lived in nursery homes in war-time London have shown how important love and attention are to the baby's psychological development, and how their absence can cause symptoms exactly like an adult psychosis. Psychiatric workers in a few experimental institutions, no-tably the Orthogenic School of the University of Chicago, have had remarkable success in rehabilitating children who were completely unable to get along at home or at school.

Until the psychologist and psychiatrist appeared on the scene, man had no scientific way of appraising himself. True, he had the great teachings of his religious leaders and the brilliant insight of his poets. But many of his

everyday opinions about himself were mutually contradictory and most of them were pessimistic about the possibility
of basic change. It was taken for granted that many men
were doomed to be unhappy, at least much of the time,
and that some were hopelessly eccentric.

The world, alas, has not yet changed a great deal. But
we already know a great deal about ourselves, and we
are learning much more. The psychologist and the psychiatrist, with their fresh approach to human nature, do
not take for granted that people are just naturally prone
to prejudice and conflict. They are not willing to concede
that some of us are born casualties, that the "nervous breakdown" is inevitable, that one man and woman out of ten will
need care in a mental hospital.

Scientists are busy learning new facts about the brain
and its chemistry, and pharmacologists are hard at work
seeking new miracle drugs for the mind—and who knows
what they may come up with? The various psychotherapists
are hard at work trying to refine and simplify what is still
the best method yet found, regardless of its disadvantages,
for understanding and relieving our emotional problems.
The psychologists are hard at work testing every assumption
of the analysts and many assumptions of their own, and
adding every day to the body of known facts about human
behavior.

Thanks to the men of the new science, we now know
more than any previous generation of mankind about the
human senses, human learning and human intelligence. We
know a good deal about our motives and our conflicts.
Our treatment of the psychologically ill is infinitely more

humane and effective than ever before. Even those of us who never took a course in psychology and never saw a psychoanalyst in the flesh are probably a little happier— a little more understanding to our wives and children, a little kinder to our associates, a little less given to superstition and prejudice about human nature. All of us, even the myriads among us who have emotional problems ranging from the light to the serious, have far more hope for the future.

« APPENDIX »

*Freudian Terms Commonly Used
by Psychoanalysts*

COMPLEX. This overused word is really nothing more than the analyst's term for any complicated and highly emotional set of attitudes and feelings. The most common ones are the Oedipus complex (the love for a parent of the opposite sex and hatred for a parent of the same sex) and the inferiority complex (a general feeling of personal inadequacy).

COMPULSION. A senseless, irresistible urge to keep performing some unnecessary act, such as eating constantly or endlessly washing the hands.

EGO. The conscious and unconscious parts of the human mind or personality which direct a person to self-preservation. Part of the ego does our logical thinking and tries to keep our lives on a sensible, even keel.

FIXATION. An arrested stage of development. A grown man who has never overcome his childish attitudes toward his mother is said to have a mother fixation.

ID. The primitive, instinctive part of the mind—our blind, unconscious, animal-like drives for fighting or for sexual satisfaction.

INHIBITION. A hidden and unconscious scruple which keeps us—often beneficially—from gratifying a desire, without our ever quite understanding why.

LIBIDO. The mental energy which we derive from our primitive sexual urges. Directed into other channels, it provides part of the drive and ambition of our lives.

OBSESSION. An insistent, nagging idea. One common form is an excessive preoccupation with neatness.

REGRESSION. The process of reverting to some childhood behavior, common among psychotics but also among fairly normal people in times of severe strain.

REPRESSION. The unconscious process of forcing unpleasant or alien thoughts or conflicts into the unconscious, so that we are not aware of or bothered by them.

SUBLIMATION. The process by which the socially and morally objectionable drives of the id are satisfied by harmless substitutes. Thus a child's urge to show off and shock people may be sublimated into a career as an actor.

SUPEREGO. Roughly, the opposite of the id. The blindly strict, stern, moralistic part of the mind or personality. It is something like the conscience—but is unconscious and unrelated to any real sense of morals or religion. It often hounds people into the most unhappy and even self-destructive conduct.

UNCONSCIOUS. The submerged, hidden part of the human mind which contains certain raw instincts plus our repressed conflicts. We are seldom aware of it, but it influences most of our behavior.

« INDEX »

111

ABOUT THE AUTHOR

WITH THE AID *of a graduate fellowship, Ernest Havemann was working toward his Ph.D. in psychology at Washington University in St. Louis when he decided to pursue a career in journalism and writing instead. He became a reporter for the St. Louis* Post-Dispatch *in 1937, and since then he has been a writer and editor for* Time *and* Life, *has contributed to* McCall's, Reader's Digest *and other magazines, and has written two books:* They Went to College *(1952), a survey of what college people are like and what becomes of them, and* I Never Thought We'd Make It *(1952), the story of an American family written in collaboration with George Love.*

Mr. Havemann's twin interests in psychology and writing were happily reunited when he was asked to write a series on psychology for Life. *These articles were published in the magazine early in 1957 and, in revised and expanded form, they are the basis for the present book.*

DATE DUE			
NOV 1 4 1974			
	DISCARDED		